CRUSH IT!

THE ART OF MARKETING YOUR BUSINESS ONLINE

KIRAN R.K.G

Book Title: CRUSH IT!

Author: KIRAN R.K.G

Published by KIRANRAJ K.G

Viraly kulathoor Uchakkada, Trivandrum, Kerala – 695506

Printed and bound by Dolfix DX-Market Pvt. Ltd. Viraly kulathoor
Uchakkada, Trivandrum, Kerala – 695506

This edition published in: 2020

ISBN 9798613589715

DEDICATION

To my Dad, who motivated me throughout my life to

become successful.

To my mom, who always supports me through all of my

crazy ideas.

To my best friends, who helped me throughout my

journey.

To, entrepreneurs all over the world who are working

hard to make this world a better place.

CONTENTS

ACKNOWLEDGEMENTS 1

INTRODUCTION 4

Alpha One ....

    Secret #1: Your Secret Clients 8

    Secret #2: The Value Ladder 15

    Secret #3: Sales Funnels 28

    Secret #4: How to Find Your Clients 47

    Secret #5: Attention Grabbers 53

    Secret #6: Types of Traffic 63

Alpha Two ....

    Secret #7: The New Marketing Funnel 71

    Secret #8: Elements of Attractive Character 81

    Secret #9: Brand Strategy 96

    Secret #10: Growth Hacking 110

    Secret #11: Spy on Your Competitors 129

    Secret #12: Funnel Hacking 177

    Secret #13: Sales Funnel Examples 193

    Secret #14: The Purple Cow 199

CONCLUSION 205

ACKNOWLEDGEMENTS

Writing a book was an awesome experience than I ever imagine. None of this would have done without the help of my best friends and family members, since they stood up and supported me throughout my entire journey, struggle and success. I'm really grateful to my dad who took extra responsibilities and takes care of our family and thought my love, respect, discipline, manners and much more to succeed in life.

To Mr. Ooman Varghese, who encouraged me throughout my adventure, he saw a kid in me who's hungry to learn, hungry to grow, and hungry to succeed

1

in business as well as life, He never stopped motivating and encouraging me. Thank you for being one of the most important people in my life.

To all those people who believed me in their journey and allowed me to implement my ideas, to find the working strategies to share them with the world.

There are lots of marketers and entrepreneurs in the world from which I learned the strategies which I'm discussing in this book and I love to specially select some of them who stood up and share their secret ideas with the world.

I like to mention a few names of marketers around the world who motivated and inspired me to write this book.

Seth Godin, Neil Patel, Russell Brunson, Gary Vaynerchuk, Dan Kennedy, Tony Robbins, Bill

Gates, Mari Smith, Larry Kim, Syed Balkhi, Susan Patel, Shama Hyder, Brian Dean, John Loomer, Mark Joyner, Jeff Walker, David Frey and everyone else who stood up to become an online entrepreneur in their life.

INTRODUCTION

'She was hated by her employer.'

Bella Adams, according to her life, was twenty-nine years old, had started her job in a reputed organization as a marketer and she was not liked by her employer since her marketing strategies always fail and she didn't deliver much value to the organization and her job doesn't last less than a year.

Bella who is in front of me today is a good marketer and a business owner of well-established and profitable business and I'm very happy for her.

I first become interested in the power of marketing seven years ago, as an entrepreneur in Kerala along the way I coordinated with lots of marketers around the globe and watched them in implementing marketing strategies in action, some of the remarkable marketing strategies and experiments in history.

We now know why most businesses fail within its first five years, How they struggle to market their products and services, and the facts behind startup mechanics. We know how to give our hands to raise them up and rebuild them according to our specifications. We understand how to make businesses to succeed in their priceless journey, market their products and services more effectively, and to make them grow dramatically.

Transforming a business isn't necessarily easy or quick. It isn't always simple.

But it's possible. And now we understand how.

This book is divided into two major parts. The first section focuses on building the right hooks to hunt your dream clients…

The second part explains how to use your clients to generate more income and the strategies which successful companies and organizations follow to dominate the market...

Each chapter revolves around a central argument: Every business and marketing strategy can become successful if we understand how it works and implements them in the right way.

ALPHA\1

SECRET #1

Your Secret Clients

It was 3:49 Am Thursday Morning, I woke up with huge head pain, I was completely stressed out no matter what I said to myself, I was not able to handle my head pain, Somehow I get out from the bed and I ended taking a tablet for this massive headache.

How had I gotten here? Before one year I had become an entrepreneur and started an online eCommerce Marketplace company, I had made a lot of mistakes along the way and learned a lot of tricks through those mistakes, the company was profitable.

A few Months Later, I started to Market more of our services in different countries, but I was shocked to see that I had a good amount of traffic on my website, but it's not converting to sales, I was wondering what's wrong with my website? Why none of this traffic is converting to sales?

I checked the product description and a lot of other factors on our website, but everything seems to be fine. I was in front of a lot of questions that need to be answered, I took a deep breath and wrote down 3 things on my whiteboard!

Who? Where? Hunt?

I asked myself,

- WHO is the person I'm looking for?
- Who're my dream customers?

- Where to find them?

- How can I make them purchase from me again and again?

I was trying to sell all my products and services to all peoples around the world, first, it seems to be a brilliant idea, but It was not. I was trying to sell our product and services who don't need it. For example: If a person wants to buy a Lamborghini and I'm trying to sell a nano car to him then what happens? Definitely, he doesn't buy it, that's what happened here.

After I find out who is my dream customers, I started to think myself about WHERE can I find them online? How can I attract them? What are their goals, dreams, and desires? How can I fulfill their dreams?

These are the questions that a company needs to solve before they go to market because most of the company starts with a product idea, they don't think about what the clients really want.

Who Is Your Client? It seems to be an interesting question for an entrepreneur.

The first question you have to ask yourself is who is your dream client? It depends upon your business it may be consumers, vendors, and associates. When a person starts a business from scratch most of the time they will not find the right client for their business they will end up feeling frustrated like I did in my early days as an entrepreneur because you're going to spend lots of time with your clients more than your own friend and family. This may let your family suffer.

I sat down in front of my laptop and I started to search on Google who my dream clients are and how they look like? After gathering a lot of ideas from

Google, I have drawn the two-person image on my whiteboard one William, who runs a clothing store and Emma who loves to purchase clothes online. I wrote about their dreams and other characteristics below their names.

Now, I have my perfect dream clients in my whiteboard, It seems silly, but It's far better to have an exact image of clients rather than a half blurred image which forms in our mind.

Where to find your clients?

Now you know who is your real clients, now it's time to find out where your dream clients are hanging around, Are they on Facebook, Snapchat, Instagram? What groups they're paired off? (Online as well as offline) Which newsletter and newspaper they read? What are their interests?

If you don't know WHO is your clients, then it's hard to find your accurate dream clients. Now note down all these pieces of information and we will use this information in the coming chapters to find the peoples you're looking for!

How you will Hunt your dream clients?

Now, we know WHO is our dream clients and where to find them, now it's time to get into Jungle and hunt our clients. To hunt these clients, you need to create something VALUABLE which attracts them it may be a Book, Video anything you like, but make sure it is valuable and it attracts you, right clients. As an online marketplace company, we conducted local events to attract persons like William and Emma. Throughout this book we will discuss how to create the right hook to attract your dream clients, now realize your hook should be something which your dream client wants.

This exercise seems to be simple, but doing it will give you more insight into your dream clients.

SECRET #2

The Value Ladder

Imagine if there is a way to increase the value of every sale in your business and it can boost your income by 40%, 160% or 300%?

The other day I met one of my friends for a coffee. We talked a lot of things, including our old school days and the events which we participated together, soon we started to discuss our businesses, He owned his business for years, he wrote an amazing business plan, and he was investing money to find new clients for his business. But the one thing he couldn't figure out is how to get more leads and conversions into his business.

Now, that's where my role comes into play, as an entrepreneur, I asked him some questions.

"How you're getting leads?" He told me that he is running Facebook Ads, Instagram Ads, and Google Ads. He was bringing a good number of leads each month.

"I told him I'm not changing anything in your lead generation strategy" He was surprised "why? I'm losing money and I'm not seeing the ROI."

I grabbed a pen and paper and drawn something which looks like a staircase.

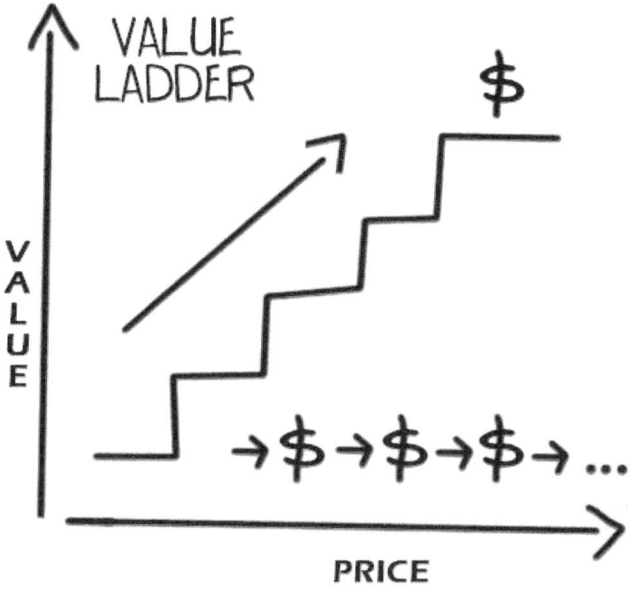

"What's that?" He asked.

I smiled and replied "It's called a Value Ladder. By using it you can retain your old customers again and again than acquiring new clients"

I had seen a lot of companies making mistakes in value ladders, They focus on how to make money instead of providing value, Remember "It's called a VALUE ladder, not a MONEY ladder" You should focus on your delivery high value for your clients. Money is secondary **"Create value for your clients the money will follow you"** most of them don't understand it but that's the fact.

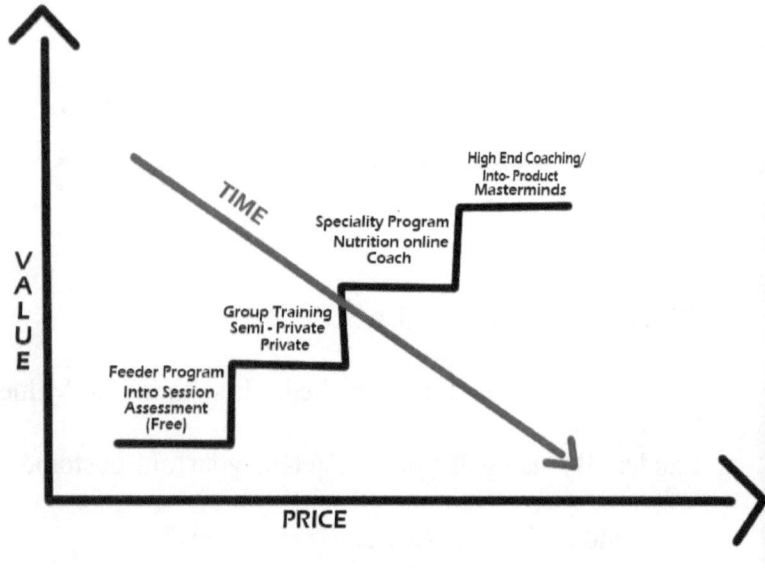

Let's discuss how to create a Value Ladder for a Fitness Business.

Your value ladder won't necessarily have

four tiers as the diagram above it all, according to you, you can use many ties as you need in your business.

TIER 1: Intro Session or Training program (Free or Low Cost)

The Goal of this tier is to grow your list and to hunt peoples who are interested in your business or services.

Some professionals don't like to give their services for free or low cost because they think it will impact their business and their credibility. Some peoples give their initial services for free so that they can build a relationship with their clients. After all, **people do business with those they know, like and trust**.

Ask yourself, you're walking through a footpath and one random person comes near you and asks for a 10k dollars will you give him? Yeah, some of them give but most of them won't but, one of your friends are asking you for a 10k dollar you will give him happily because you trust him, you know him, there is a relationship between you two, the same scenario is applied to your online business.

TIER 2: Group Training or workshops

Tier 2 focuses to increase your profits and trusts with your clients. This mid-range services you offer generates more profit and build trust since they receive more value from your business.

TIER 3: Private Training

These are mid-range services that you can offer your dream clients to increase your revenue. You can use start membership and continuity programs for recurring revenue. It's better to have two to four-person model because more than that will feel like small group coaching

TIER 4: Gold Training

This is your top tier where you're going to deliver the biggest and the best services you have. If you offer 1hour sessions, then you can take seven to nine sections daily, you can increase this by increasing the number of trainers or by reducing the time of sections. This will help you to generate more conversions from your existing clients.

Imagine a scenario where you have to sell only one product to one customer at a time with no new, old, or returning customers. Imagine one more scenario where your clients want to spend only a hundred dollars with you when you're aiming for a thousand dollars.

That's why most of the businesses go bankrupt in less than two years. These businesses don't have a value leader

Let's see some of the value ladders that businesses follow which makes more than five figures a month.

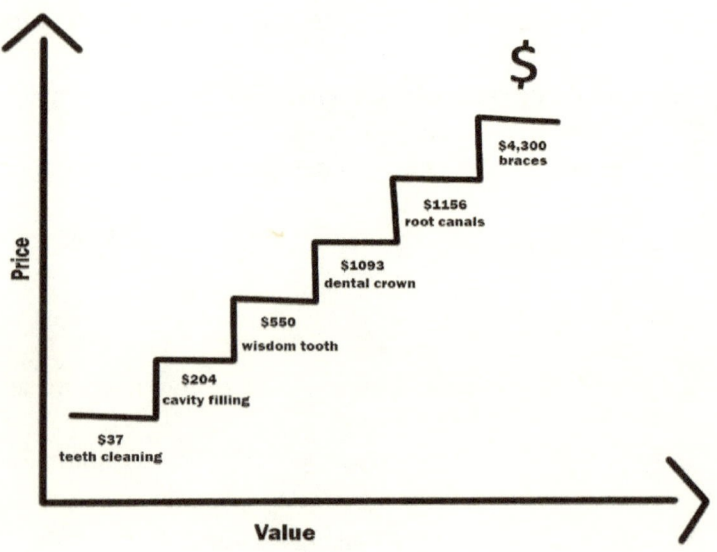

The value ladder which is shown above is used by a Dentists to hunt more clients and to make them repeat customers.

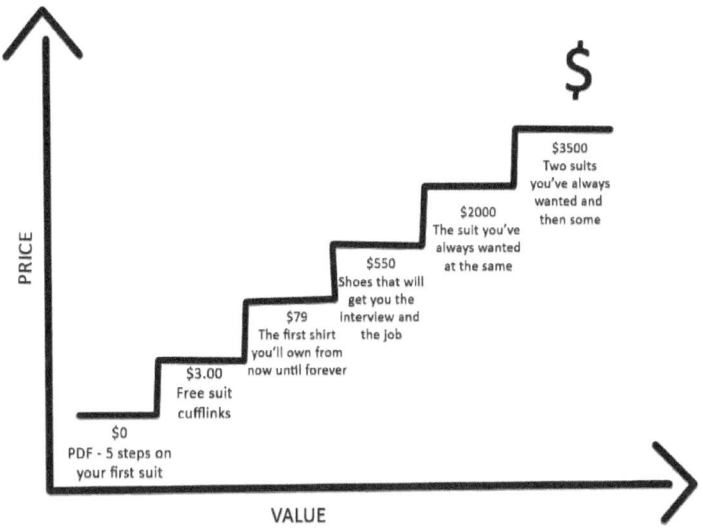

The value ladder which is used by Tailors

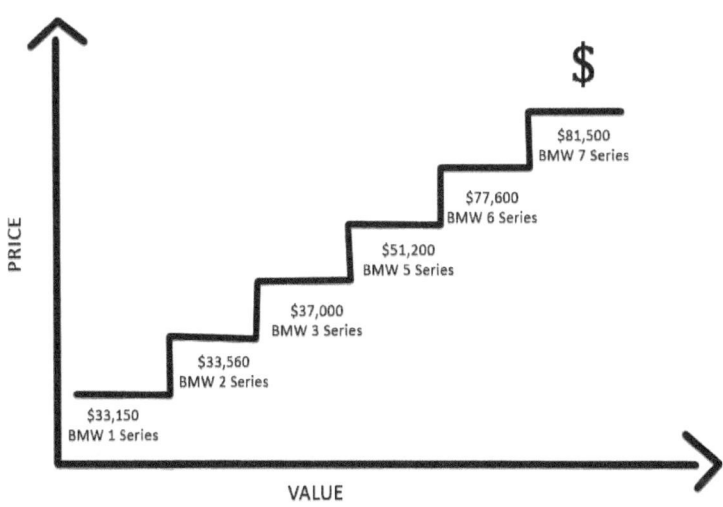

The value ladder which is followed by BMW

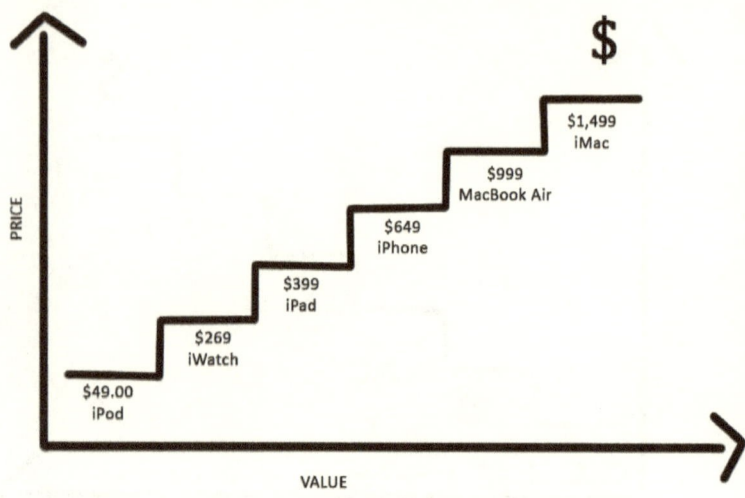

The Value Ladder which is followed by Apple

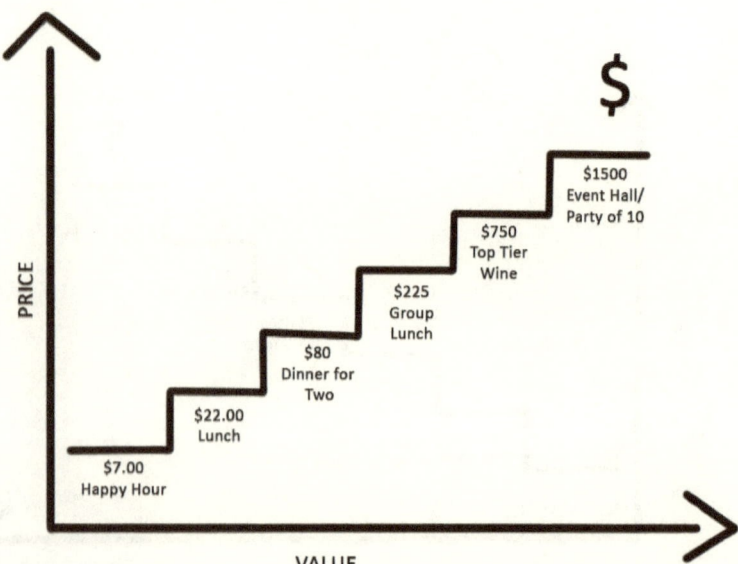

The value ladder which is used by a Restaurant or a Bar

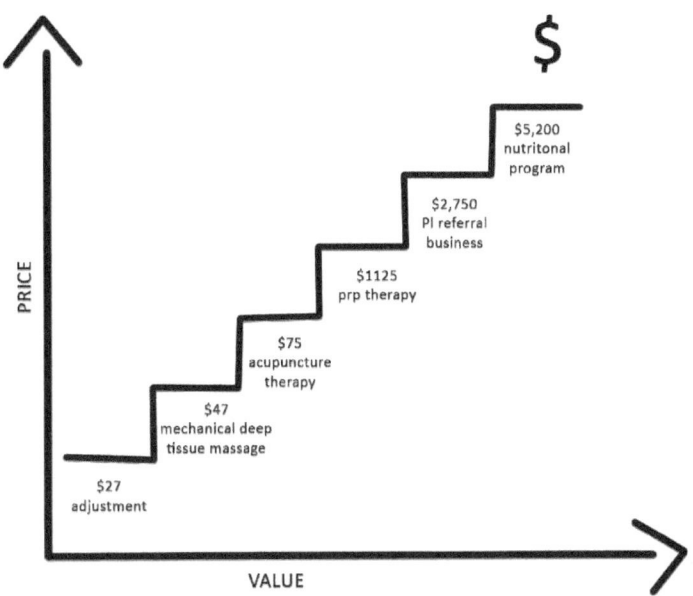

$

PRICE

$5,200
nutritonal
program

$2,750
PI referral
business

$1125
prp therapy

$75
acupuncture
therapy

$47
mechanical deep
tissue massage

$27
adjustment

VALUE

The value ladder which is used by a Chiropractor

There are lots of different ways you can build your value ladder. You need to focus more on your clients what they really want from your products or services?

Now it's time to make your own value ladder for your business. Please think and fill up the value ladder below.

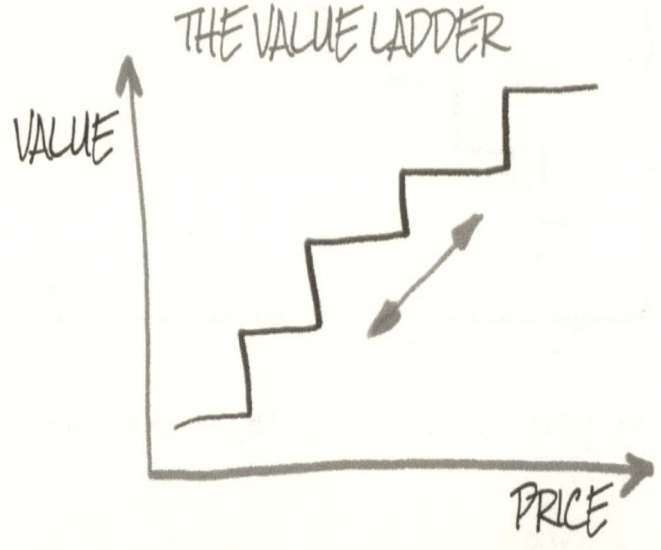

In the next chapter, we're going to discuss the basics of sales funnels it's important to create your value ladder unless you have a value ladder you can't create a sales funnel.

SECRET #3

Sales funnels

The first secret which I discussed with you is to find out who are your dream clients? Where to find them? And the second secret I discussed with you is what is a value ladder? and how can you make one for your business? In this chapter, we will discuss what is a sales funnel? Why should you need one for your business?

Sales funnels are the backbone to market your product or services, If you're a beginner in sales funnels you may find it so messy and difficult to understand, don't worry, I will break it down for you. Yes, it is possible to have fun with sales funnels, I will show you how!

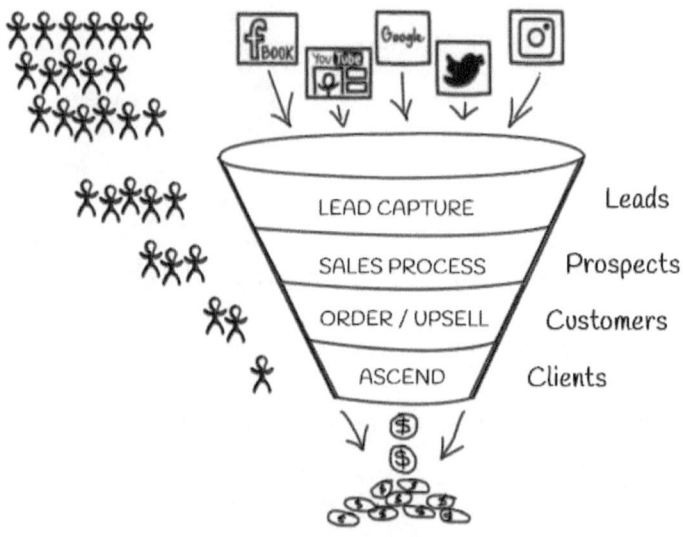

To get more sales for your product or services first you need to bring traffic to your website or landing page If you're trying to sell your product or services through a single web page than you're going to disappoint because one single page is not enough to engage new clients or expensive products or services.

The top of the sales funnel is where you're going to bring traffic usually from social media ads and through public blogs, once your dream clients are in your sales funnel, we need to engage with them using influenceable content to finish the sale at the end of sales funnel.

This process is called a "sales funnel".

I had seen lots of sponsored ads throughout my carrier most of them are not engaged, when you create an ad for your product or a service make sure to create an ad which can engage with your audience because most people in social media is not there to purchase your products or services they are there to network and entertain themselves. So, make sure to create an ad that engages with your right audience, it's always best to create video ads. I personally prefer YouTube video ads because of the cheap and converts than Facebook ads. If you're going for a Facebook ad then make sure to run a split test campaign (also known as A/B testing) on the Facebook ad manager and find out which ad is performing well in it and use that ad to drive traffic to your landing page or website.

Every successful business has a powerful sales funnel it's invisible to your naked eyes in comping chapters I will explain to you how to find and reverse hack these funnels so that you can make a more powerful sales funnel than your competitor has used use it against them to earn more money.

Sales funnels are everywhere, but you don't notice it

Every business has their own sales funnels,

Yeah is not surprising, even "Your business has your own sales funnel, but you don't reorganize it, if you recognize it, then you have much more control and influence over it" Website optimization matters when it comes to your sales funnel and every stage of it has an impact on your client, you need to know them immediately.

Let's see an example of a Brick and mortar sales funnel

It was time for my brother's wedding, before two months of the ceremony we decided to purchase some new clothes. I took my family members to one of the big shopping malls in my city, After entering the shopping mall, we started to browse some wedding suits for my brother. After one minute a sales representative came near us and offer us her assistance.

She has shown us some of the best suit collections available on that mall and I liked one of the designs.

I asked my brother "how is this suit?" He replied "it's Good, I liked it"

Sales Representative "Sir, we have a discount going on now, if you're taking two suits from this brand you will get one suit for free of your choice"

I and my brother have thought for a while, my brother said "It seems to be a fair deal"

I replied "yeah, let us take two suits"

We were impressed by the offer and took 2 shots and chose one free suit. Then at the point of sale, the sales representative recommends some watch collections they have which look nice with the suits. We browse through all those watch collections and ended up adding two watches in our shopping cart. We were so happy with the suits and watch we bought.

It was not over there, we were so pleased with the deal, on the next day I recommended the mall to my friend and we have gone to buy some suits for him.

The same process plays on your website in the placement of sales associate you have pages to help and guide your website traffic through the sales funnel. Understanding your sales funnel can help you to find and fix the holes in it. Remember that you can **"Influence how visitors move through the funnel and whether they eventually convert"**

You might be wondering your website is getting lots of traffic but most of the visits and drop off, why they drop off? This can be a number of reasons, it can be a technical error, might be your website loading time, disconnects between your ad and your landing page and so on. Each of these drop-offs will increase your bounce rate and lowers the conversion rate. When you build your sales funnel, you will learn how to identify and fix the "Leaks." So that more and more of your traffic became loyal customers.

Sales Funnel Explained

When a visitor lands on your website through social media or by any search engines, He or she is now a prospect, The visitor might check out a few of your blogs or browse through the product listings and services you offer, At a certain point you offer him chance to sign up for your email list. If a visitor fills out your form, then the visitor becomes a lead. You can use those pieces of information to market your product or services via email, phone or text. You can use offers to bring them back to your website

The sales funnels narrow as traffic moves through it because you will have more traffic at the top of the funnel than buyers at the bottom,

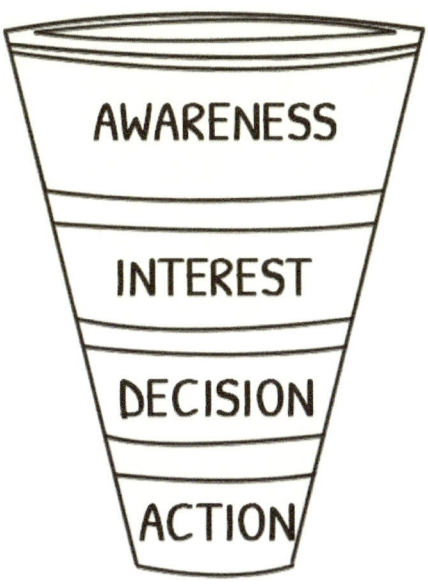

Awareness

This is where you hunt a client, it might be from Twitter, Facebook, Google or any other platforms. At this stage, the prospect learns about your products or services. They might also become aware of the problems that they need to solve and the possible ways to deal with it.

Interest

When consumers reach this stage in the sales funnel, they're doing active research, comparison shopping, and thinking about their options. This is the time where you show incredible content that helps them with their problems but doesn't sell your products or services to them. If you're trying to sell your product or service from the initial stage then you will chase them away, the goal here is to establish a relationship and to show your expertise, With your content you need to help the client to make an informed decision and to help them in any way you can.

The best organic way to increase awareness and interest is through blogging.

Decision

At this stage, the client is ready to buy the product or services from you, but they might be considering more than one option, including you. This is the best time to make your offer. It can be offered like discounts, a lower price than the competitor, bonus products or services. Whatever the case, make it so irresistible that your client can't wait to take advantage of it.

Action

This is the very bottom of your sales funnel, where your client assets, he may purchase your products or services and becomes a part of your business. You want to do your best to turn one purchase, into 20, 200, 400 and so on.

In this stage, you need to keep your customers happy by giving your best product and services and make them repeat customers and brand advocates, Word of Mouth is a powerful force and no one can do it better than a happy client.

Remember this truth:

"Satisfied customer is the best source of advertisement" - Philip Kotler

You can conduct Webinars to help a client to

decide and take action for your products or services. You can use videos in all the four stages of the sales funnel, YouTube is known as the second largest search engine, so by optimizing the videos for certain keywords, you can generate tons of awareness and traffic to your website

Best Sales Funnel Example

CRAZYEGG.COM

Crazy Egg's sales funnel is huge and they have excellent blogs with high-quality content, their sales funnel starts from their blogs. Most of their traffic is coming from search engines like Google.

They have a Call To Action (CTA) at the bottom of their blog posts to drive customers onto their email list.

Steps in Sales Funnel

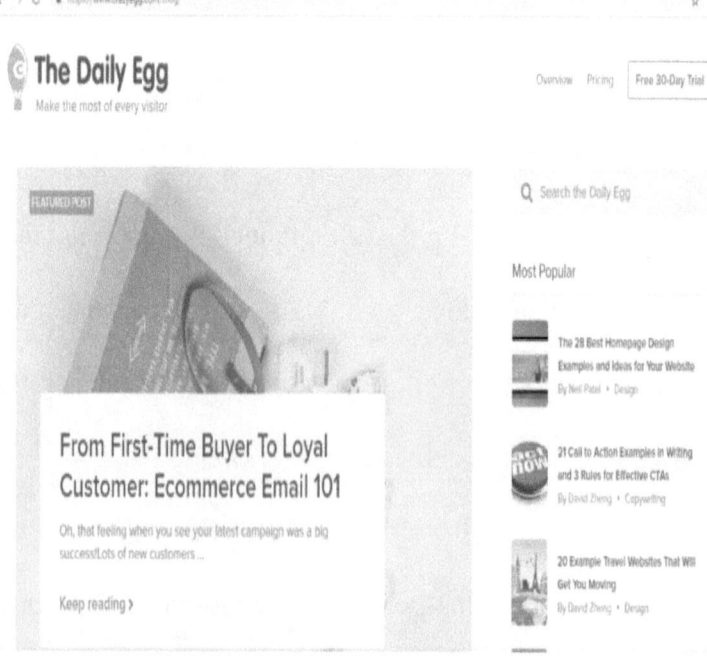

- Traffic (from blogs, Ads, organic, referrals)

- Crazy Egg has a pop-up at the bottom of their blog posts for a free 30-day trial, if you sign up for the email list, you will be brought back to their homepage.

- They have linked directly to Crazy Egg at the top of every page

- Homepage (email and password required for the next step) simple as that.

Pricing Plan

Checkout form

Start Your Free 30-Day Trial

View Your Heatmap & Get Started in Less Than 60 Seconds.

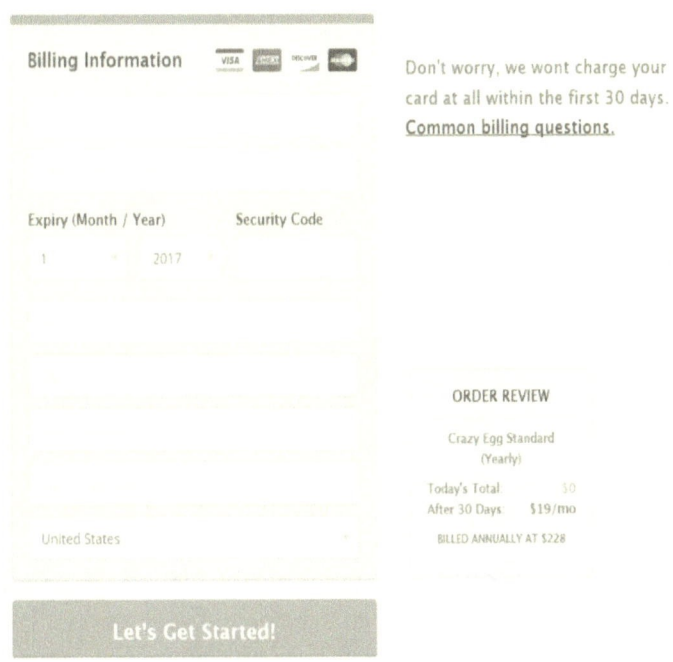

The pricing page looks similar to the rest of the site. It's very simple and has been like this for over a year now. They offer free trials; the pricing page has a light copy with social proof and the language used throughout the website is simple.

After selecting your pricing plan, the final step is to add billing information, Crazy Egg assures you on the checkout page that you won't be charged within the first 30 days.

Why does it work?

According to Neil Patel, The Founder of Crazy Egg. Crazy Egg has consistently doubled its conversions and revenue year over year.

The focus of the funnel's design is on simplicity. There's not a lot of copy. Instead, there's a focus on strong visuals.

What Makes it Unique?

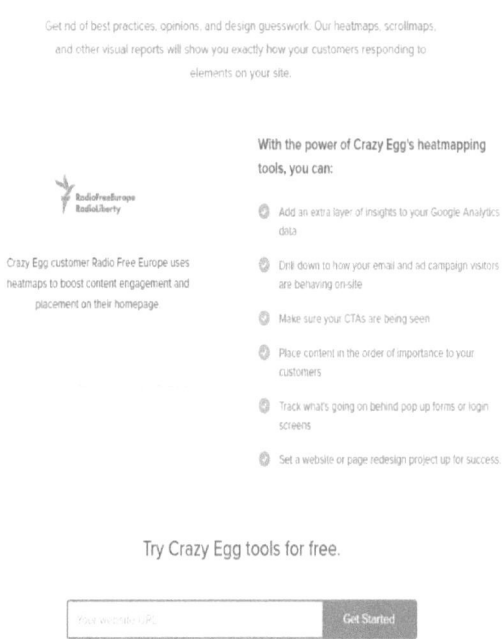

Get rid of best practices, opinions, and design guesswork. Our heatmaps, scrollmaps, and other visual reports will show you exactly how your customers responding to elements on your site.

With the power of Crazy Egg's heatmapping tools, you can:

Crazy Egg customer Radio Free Europe uses heatmaps to boost content engagement and placement on their homepage

- Add an extra layer of insights to your Google Analytics data
- Drill down to how your email and ad campaign visitors are behaving on-site
- Make sure your CTAs are being seen
- Place content in the order of importance to your customers
- Track what's going on behind pop up forms or login screens
- Set a website or page redesign project up for success.

Try Crazy Egg tools for free.

Get Started

Instead of bombarding the customer with information. Crazy Egg keeps the info light and simple. However, the copy is clear and confident, so customers know what they're getting before they submit their email address.

Let's Review: The sales funnel is the path

that an online visitor takes through your website that results in conversions. Because the amount of traffic your website gets will be larger, with prospects dropping off at various points in that path, those that do convert will be a smaller percentage of the original traffic-That's why it's a funnel shape.

Up Next: So, the next question will be WHERE do you find your peoples to put into your sales funnel? The next chapter will help you to hunt your dream clients and bring them to your website with their money wallets.

SECRET #4

How to Find Your Clients

Now you have a complete idea about who you're dreaming clients are. Now you may be wondering WHERE to find them online and how can you bring them to your website? I'm going to break that secret for you in this chapter.

If you had gone through Secret 1 and Secret 2 and done your homework, then finding your dream clients are going to be easier than you think. The clearer you're with your dream clients the more benefits and conversions you get when you interact with them.

Where your dream clients "HANG OUT"?

If you had done the proper research about WHO is your dream clients, then you will have a very good idea about WHERE they hang out online? Which social groups did they follow? What are their interests & behaviors? And what they're acting searching and planning? Thanks to Mark Zuckerberg through his platforms like (Facebook, Instagram, and other social platforms) you can find your dream clients and put an Ad in front of them easily.

On a Sunday morning, I was traveling to my home town, It was a wonderful journey since I got a new friend, Dave as a travel companion. He loves fishing and he teaches his students how to fish in the oceans. It was really amazing hearing about his ocean adventures. Soon our discussion diverted to sharks,

I asked him "Do you ever catch a shark?"

Dave: smiled and said, "Yeah, I did and I teach my students to do so, but after the learning section we will release the shark back to the ocean."

I was really amazed, that I got a friend who catches sharks. I was so curious, I wanted to know more about shark hunting.

I asked him How you understand WHERE to fish these sharks in the ocean?

Dave: "finding the right place to hunt the shark is critical, we always start with areas of structures like wrecks, holes, and ledges."

I asked Dave, "How you attract the shark what type of bait you use for it?"

Dave replied: "We fish with lots of standard shark

baits like bluefish and mackerel"

I asked: "Why bluefish and mackerel?"

Dave: "These fishes are oily they attract the sharks."

It was really amazing to learn new facts about oceans through Dave. Here, In the case of Dave his clients were "Sharks," he had a good understanding about WHERE they CONGREGATING so he gone to the exact spot in the ocean and use a perfect bait to hunt the sharks. As a Marketer, your icon is the Internet and your bait is Ads and your dream clients are sharks.

You can use social media like Facebook to create an Ad that targets the exact clients you're searching for. On Facebook, you can use Demographics and Psychographics to filter out your custom audience.

Demographics are statistical facts about your clients, such as:

- How old they are
- Their ethnicity or race
- Their gender
- Their income
- What level of education they have?

Psychographics, on the other hand, are:

- Attitudes
- Aspirations
- Interests
- Opinions
- Behaviors

Facebook has a lot of data about peoples you can use them as your advantage in your Business.

First of all, your dream clients should know your business exits, Secondly, they need to know you can help them to get their problem solved.

Remember this Truth:

"A problem is a chance for you to do your best" -

Duke Ellington

The best way to know you exist and make them work with you is by providing the educational content which solves their problems. Always make sure to keep them free and don't try to sell anything when you're educating them it will chase them away to your competitors.

Get your best content in front of your clients

Now you know where your dream clients are hanging around and what problems they're currently facing, now it's time for placing Ads in front of them like Dave used a perfect bait to attract the sharks. When you give free educational content, make sure to collect people's contact details (name and email) so that you can use these pieces of information to follow up with them in the future.

SECRET #5

Attention Grabbers

Now you know WHERE to find your dream clients, Now the question is:

How can you attract them so that they leave the place where they're congregating and check your website/landing page?

If you don't pay any attention to marketing, A study reported by Psychology Today states that the average American sees or hears 3,700+ Ads and marketing messages a day. Sounds Interesting right? When I wake up every morning and until I reach back to my home, I probably see or hears over 6,000 advertising messages. Depending upon where my day takes me.

Let us see an example of turnstiles on the New York subway.

If you look at the image you can find advertisings on the lower part of the turnstile, Now Look into the image once again you will see advertised on the turnstile bars.

Large companies spend millions of dollars to find different ways of grabbing your attention, They work with brilliant marketers all over the work of planning and executing different ways to grab your attention towards their brands, Some of them hire different companies and together they spend tons of hours in meetings creating ads so you pay attention to their brands rather paying attention to their competitors. If you're a small business enterprise or a Marketing manager working in a mid-sized company then you don't have to spend money on marketing as larger organizations do. But you should find the right way to grab the attention of your dream clients.

How easy is it to grab people's attention?

Before starting my online Marketplace company, I used to travel and attend different trade shows which are conducted all over the world. One of them was really awesome.

The show had more than 7 halls and it was hard to differentiate between one booth from another.

For me, almost all clothing booths looked the same, many of them used young, beautiful women to gather people's attention. But one of the booths was different they used this tactic to catch my attention.

Yeah, it's a Lamborghini in the booth, they conducted fashion shows and allowed customers to take pictures with it and given them offers to purchase clothes from their booth. And it worked like hell, I was stunned by seeing the marketing strategy.

I can understand that you can't put a full-size Lamborghini in your website, so when you create your website you should make sure to grab people's attention by

- Images
- Sounds
- Videos
- Words
- Illustrations

If you're working on your website then your job is to get people's attention so they continue their reading.

Headlines

If you want to bring more traffic to your website by an Ad then you MUST have an attention-grabbing headline in it.

When you create an Ad with just an Image, words or videos may impress people sometimes it might catch their attention, but it will not bring traffic to your website if you don't have a headline.

The perfect headline will catch a reader's attention in

less than 3sec

You can use one of these headline types:

- How-to (How to Be Thin)
- News style (Woman Loses 23 Pounds in 10 Minutes)
- Benefit (Weight Loss the Easy Way)
- Explanatory (How Fast Slim Speeds Weight Loss)
- Testimonial ("I LOVE Fast Slim So Much!")
- Direct Offer (45% Off, Fast Slim Today)

• Guarantee (Lose 23 Pounds in 10 Minutes or Get Your Money Back)

When you create a headline make sure to be as specific as possible, headlines can be short or several lines use a pre-head, which is a short headline above the main headline. It's also called an 'eyebrow' and you can use the word Attention. (ATTENTION: Fat People!) And You can also use a sub-head or bullets (or both) directly below the main headline.

Videos

Videos are an awesome tool for creating and expanding your brand awareness. They always drive traffic to your website from social media, then image Ads. Videos will engage with your custom audience. You can also add videos on your landing pages. Many peoples don't like to read all contents on your landing pages, Videos will work best for those peoples.

When you include a video on a landing page make sure to it's relevant to the sales message and it should tell the reader to keep reading. Include a tease like, "in the message below, you're going to discover exciting news about losing weight quickly and safely."

In reality, that's not a tease, but a headline!

Images

Many sponsored ads and landing pages work without any images at all. However, much of my copy includes an attention-grabbing image next to the headline.

- You can use the photo of the expert who is the 'author' of the message.
- Before-and-after photos work well for some products, especially in the health space.
- You can use a "crazy" image that really has little

to do with the product or service but makes the reader laugh or wince.

- Some marketers believe a celebrity will help them get your attention.
- Others like to use photos of dogs or smiling children.
- When in doubt, show happiness or the end result.

Tip: When you create a Video or an Image Ad make sure to add your logo to any of the corners of the Post-it will attract your dream clients and increase your branding.

Your ads should establish curiosity to your audience, it will increase the flow of traffic to your website or landing page.

No matter what attention grabbers you use for your business it worth to test them so you discover what works best for your business.

Remember this Truth:

"The real fact of the matter is that nobody reads ads.

People read what interests them, and sometimes it's an ad." – Howard Luck Gossage

Up Next: In the next chapter, we will discuss different types of traffic.

SECRET #6

Types of Traffic

There are a lot of ways to describe different types of traffic, Today I'm going to break it down into three categories.

1. **Traffic You Influence**
2. **Traffic You Rent**
3. **Traffic You Own**

Traffic You Influence

Influenced traffic is the traffic that you can't control, but you can influence it. The best example of influence traffic is the traffic which you get from Google and from other social media, If your websites and blogs rank higher in Google then you will get more and more influenced traffic.

Having presence in all social media is a plus point, You can't directly control whether peoples will like your page on Facebook or follow you on twitter, and visit your website from there to become your customer, but if you post engaging contents in your social media, you can build your audience and many of them will become your new clients.

The influenced traffic, which is coming from Google to your blog post, make sure to collect their email address by using a popup on your blogs. It will help you to build your email list and those peoples who are subscribed will become your new leads (THE TRAFFIC YOU OWN)

If you're an entrepreneur who is struggling financially or small-sized business then I highly recommend starting with influences traffic, because it's completely free of cost.

Tip: To rank higher in Google you should focus on your SEO, website loading time, the website should be Desktop and Mobile friendly and make sure your website is working in HTTPS protocol.

Traffic You Rent

From the name itself, you can understand you're renting traffic from one place to your landing page, which means you're advertising your product or services online on different platforms to attract new clients.

There are a lot of companies which is offering advertising services some of them are: Google Ads, Bing Ads, Facebook Ads, LinkedIn Ads, Twitter Ads and a lot more. You can also use radio, Podcasts, direct mail, and other services.

The best thing about advertising is that you have full control of your Ads, you can decide where it should appear online, once you follow the best advertising practices, then your ads will deliver good quality traffic to your website.

Traffic You Own

This is the actual traffic you own, the best example of it is an Email Newsletter. Here you have the full control over the timing of the messages you send to your subscribers, if you have a huge subscriber list, then you'd already have all the traffic you need to sustain your business.

Tip: You can use push notifications on your website to notify users when you publish a new blog post or when you're providing offers for your products or services. It will help you to bring the traffic you own into your website again and again as a newsletter does.

 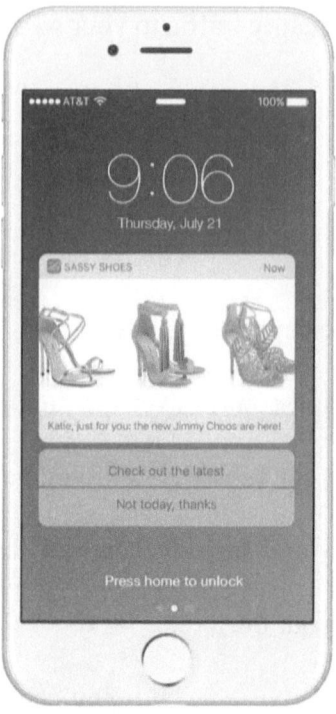

As a business owner or a Marketer, you should always think about how can you change the Influenced traffic and the Rented traffic to The Traffic your own.

Your highest priority should be to convert the Influenced traffic and Rented traffic to the

TRAFFIC YOU OWN.

Remember this Truth:

"Today it's not about 'getting the traffic' – it's about 'getting the targeted and relevant traffic.'" – Adam Audette

ALPHA 2

SECRET #7

The New Marketing Funnel

In secret #3 we had discussed, how to build your sales funnel, personally I like to call it an old-school funnel. I will tell you why?

The Old-School Funnel

This marketing funnel version required you to continually fill the top of the funnel with as many people as possible from the bottom of the funnel only filters out a small percentage of customers.

The old-school sales funnel looked like this:

And was supposed to act like this:

It's time to throw that old-school funnel out of the window.

Reason: With the cone-shaped funnel you will always try to acquire new customers and once a client purchases your products or services your job is done. It's not a good strategy for growth.

Now it's time to introduce you to a new funnel design, which looks like a bow tie that's wide on left and right and narrow in the middle.

The New Marketing Funnel

Customer relationships are the strategies and tactics to get, keep and grow customers.

- **Getting clients** is sometimes called demand creation, drives clients in your chosen sales channel.
- **Keeping clients** and retaining them will give them a reason to stick with your business and with your products or services.
- **Growing clients** involve selling your products and services to your dream clients and encourages them to refer new clients.

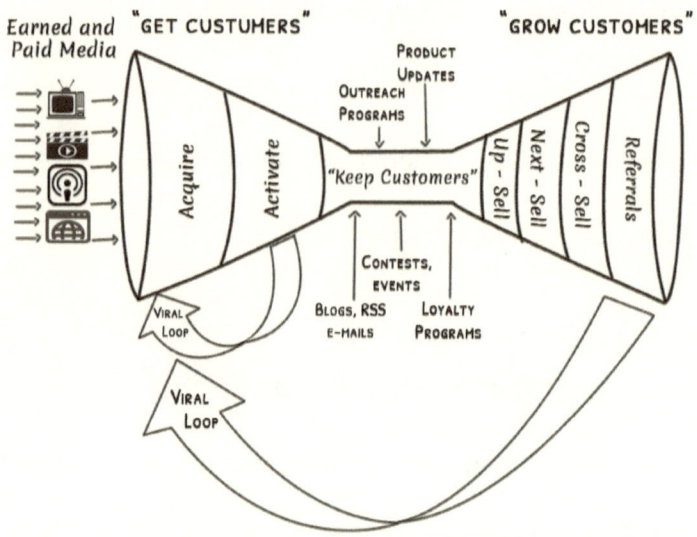

The above image shows the entire client relationship life cycle. The "Get, Keep & Grow" are among the most important factors for any business.

Keep Customers

As a business owner or as a Marketer you should think about how you're going to retain your clients which you worked hard to acquire. It's always cheaper to keep your clients than acquiring new clients again and again.

To make the process simple you must deliver your clients with high value and the promises that you make. Your dream clients should love your products, services, and the support which you're giving for your products or services.

The company should take feedbacks and be innovative to make upgrades and changes to the products or services to stay ahead of the competition.

Loyalty Programs: You should focus to make your clients happy by conducting loyalty programs like points, rewards, discounts or multiple year contracts. You should make sure that your existing customers are happy with you, otherwise, you will risk losing them to your competitors.

Client check-ins: Plan to call or email your

clients once a month to thank them for their business and see how they're getting on. Take feedbacks for your products and services, if a new client is dropping out without purchasing your products or services, then contact them to know why, and bring them abroad by giving offers and discounts. Email is commonly used for these purposes, but I highly recommend to contact your clients through a phone call because nothing beats the personal touch like a phone call. When you call a person and provide a personal touch, you're building a relationship and credibility. (If you have a sales team make sure to train them with a good sales script before calling any of your clients).

Most importantly, reach out to people who post bad reviews about your products or services, understand why, and try to improve their experience with your business. There are hundreds of tools out there that help you to track behaviors and customer cycles. Start measuring those metrics. These facts are applicable in your offline business too, check your CCTV and monitor where people go and what they took and purchased from you. Look at the trends of each day, month, seasonal, etc. There is no excuse for not understanding your clients.

Remember this Truth:

"Your most unhappy customers are your greatest source of learning."- Bill Gates

Grow your Clients

The most common mistake which startup companies make is, they always focus on their revenue which they receive in their initial sales, but the smart startups think about the revenue they can get over the lifetime. (Lifetime value),

There are two major parts that help your business to grow faster, they're getting clients to buy more and also refer, recommend and share your products or services to others.

Cross-Sell: Encourage buyers of a product to buy adjacent products, this is the example "people who brought this, also brought', the section of Amazon.

Up-Sell: Promote your clients to purchase higher-end products. The most commonly seen example of this is services or packages with a tiered price and feature list.

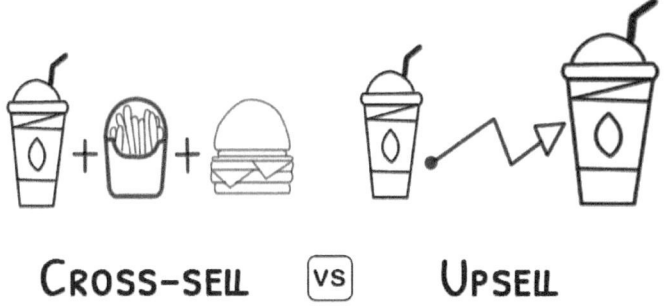

CROSS-SELL [vs] UPSELL

Next Sell: Concentrate on your next order: encourage your clients for a long-term contract, sell additional products and services by finding and solving the problems which your clients are facing, and become your client's primary seller. These strategies work well in eCommerce.

Unbundling: focus to increase revenue, if your product is multi-featured, then split it into several products, sell them separately. This works well in tech and software businesses.

Referrals: focus for word of mouth

marketing, because no marketing strategy can beat word of mouth marketing. This will encourage your clients to talk as much as possible about your brand and services.

If your organization is well established or you have sufficient financial background, then you can pay your clients for referring new clients as Uber did in its initial days. Pay the clients who are referring and pay the new clients when they sign up for your services from a referral link, this will give a boost to your word of the mouth marketing.

Get these strategies right, you will end up creating a viral loop for your business.

SECRET #8

Elements of the Attractive Character

I had a client who I had recently undertaken the process of building a value ladder and sales funnel, he had so many questions about sales and marketing and one of the main questions was the concept of "Attractive Character" and how to implement it into his business.

In this chapter, we will discuss the concept of Attractive character and why should you need one in your business.

Story + Message + Values + Brand Identity =

Attractive Character

If you need to establish a personal connection with your dream clients, then Attractive character is a must for your business, An Attractive Character helps you to make a real connection and let your clients know you better.

Attractive Character is simply positioning yourself or a publicly known figure as your brand Identity

In my childhood I and my brother loved to watch Teenage Mutant Ninja Turtles, I was a great fan of Donatello (The purple turtle) and my brother loved Raphael (The red turtle), In my childhood, I was so crazy that I always try to intimate the characters in TV shows. One day I got a bamboo stick in my hand from that day, I started to act like Donatello, it was really amazing and Wonderful moments in my childhood, I started using the boo to fight with my brother.

The crazy part is people stop watching their favorite shows when something happens to their favorite character. If you know the series, Walking dead you may know what happened to Glenn he was brutally killed, and the ratings of the show plummeted. I personally believe if something happened to Raphael or Donatello, we should have stopped watching the show.

We all have a favorite character, right? Why

do we have one? How they become our favorite characters? The fact is, we always like to relate ourselves to these characters due to shared characteristics, personalities, and character flaws.

The fictional character becomes more powerful when you use it on your business When you use a fictional character in your email or sales letter people will get involved in everything that fictional character does. This attractive character is used to narrate the story that leads to your products or services and inspires your dream clients to take action.

Components of an Attractive Character

The main pieces of an Attractive Character are the elements, the identity, and the storyline. First, we will look into the elements of an attractive character.

- **Your Backstory**

- **Parables**
- **Character Flaws**
- **Polarity**

Element #1 - Your Backstory

Your backstory should be something which lets peoples more about you and you have to tell them how you came into the position of knowing what you do and why you're the go-to authority for what you offer.

Element #2 - Use Parables

I personally like to use parables a lot. Which is the exact way of storytelling, which has some meaning at the end that people can associate with a session that can be learned?

Parables and stories are like bridges for our memory, that's why parables a great way for people to remember the story and why it's important to do what you're saying.

Fables vs. Parables

Fable	Parable
• A brief story illustrating a moral or revealing general truths about human nature	• A short story designed to allegorically teach some religious principle, moral lesson, or general truth
• Often include talking animals or animated objects as the principal characters	• Includes real or literal occurrences to which anyone can relate

Element #3 -Character Flaws

When it comes to character, you should not be perfect because no one likes and follows a perfect person. People always follow others who are approachable and have been where they have been. They want to follow someone that knows the pain which they're struggling with and can lead them to overcome them.

For example, my character flaw: I'm not smart, I'm a college dropout, I don't have a well financial background, I've had a few businesses that were seven figures before and they failed, I worked and got back up, I pushed myself and kept pushing ahead. Once I discover Marketing and the power of sales everything fell into place, now I have been able to build six and seven-figure empires.

So those are my character flaws, I'm not intelligent, I'm not perfect, I had failed a number of times, Every successful person has failed at some point, but by continues learning from others, we can fail less, By following my advice you can skip all those mistakes which I did in my past and be successful as I'm.

Element #4 - Be Polarizing

Polarity means you want your dream clients to choose aside. If you say Are you a leader or a follower?", "Are you male or female" These are all polarizing questions because they immediately place someone in a box or make them chose aside.

The more you polarize, the more that someone either says yes or no to you, the more that you are caving the path for your dream clients. The people will loyally, follow you and love everything you produce, So polarizing your audience is the best way to create a following of people that love what you're about & make more money.

Identity of an Attractive Character

Below is a list of four most identifiable, attractive characters, you can use them build your Attractive Character.

The Leader

The leader is someone who will be leading their audience from one place to another. The leader shares the same story as their audience and has most likely overcome all the problems he faced on his way. The audience will look up to the leader as someone who can solve their problems.

The Adventurer/Crusader

The adventurer is the curious type. They don't have all the answers but will be more than willing to go find the answer and bring back other golden nuggets of treasure along the way, The Adventurer is similar to a leader, but instead of leading their audience along the path, they will help find the answers.

The Reporter/Evangelist

The reporter is someone who hasn't traveled the path and found all the answers. So, they put on their decorative hats and go uncover the truths to share with their audience. This usually happens in the way of interviews and articles.

The Reluctant Hero

The classic reluctant hero. Think Harry Potter, he's a shy boy who doesn't want to be in the spotlight. But what he uncovers brings him this moral obligation to do what's right and share his discoveries about 'you know who'.

The spotlight is uncomfortable, but you know you need to be there. This can be a very powerful persona.

Attractive Character Storylines

These are the ways in which we communicate with our audience. This can be done through landing pages, emails, videos, etc.

LOSS AND REDEMPTION

This storyline follows the path a person having it all, then BAM! They lose everything and have to work their way out of the mess they're in, but in the end, they actually learned so much and want to share it with you.

US VS THEM

This takes us back to 'Polarity'. The storyteller will gather with their audience and bring them closer and realizing their enemies.

BEFORE AND AFTER

These are stories of transformation about how the storyteller was like 'a' and now after taking 'this product' or 'this course', they are now like 'b'. These are generally self-explanatory and the easiest stories to tell.

AMAZING DISCOVERY

These stories are told with enthusiasm and get the audience excited about what you have to share with them. It can be about a special product or about a company or person who's made your life better.

SECRET TELLING

By having a secret and promising to share it

with the audience in return for their details can be a powerful hook. People by nature are inquisitive and love being involved in a secret. It's a great way to bring people through the steps of your funnel.

3RD PERSON TESTIMONIAL

You don't even have to tell a story about yourself. A testimonial from someone is a very powerful selling tool indeed. The more testimonials, the better. This gives social proof and the reassurance most people need.

So, there you have it! All of this can seem like a lot of work and not worth the effort, but if you just sit down and write down the outline of your attractive character, it will help you massively during your sales process. Do not underestimate the power of the attractive character.

SECRET #9

Brand Strategy

Your brand is your reputation, it's what people say about your business when you're not around. Your brand has mainly two types of reputation, The first one is a general review where people say "They're the best company" another one is "They're expert in a specific field" from my experience the business which is expertise in a specific field gets more referrals than the first one. Another important aspect of a brand is its visibility into how well known is your organization in your target market.

The better your visibility and reputation the stronger your brand will be.

Brand strategy is a plan which helps organizations to achieve their long-term goals through the evolution of its successful brand. When we talk about branding everyone thinks it's all about products, services, website, logo or organization name but the fact is your brand is much more than that, because the best brand is all about establishing feelings and emotions with their target audience.

Remember this truth:

"Making promises and keeping them is a great way to build a brand" - Seth Godin

Components of a comprehensive branding strategy

Purpose

You should understand what your business promises, and your purpose should be a different form of your competitors.

"Every brand makes a promise. But in a marketplace in which consumer confidence is low and budgetary vigilance is high, it's not just making a promise that separates one brand from another, but having a definite purpose" - **Allen Adamson**

Consistency

When you talk about your business, make sure you don't confuse your audience, it's better you don't take anything that doesn't relate to your brand.

When you add a new post on any social platforms, try to post something which is relevant for your business, don't try to add posts that are funny, Franky, etc. Because it will confuse your audience, to attract the right audience and to keep the existing audience you should make sure your message is cohesive, This will create more brand recognition and boosts customer loyalty.

The best example of consistency is Coca-Cola Brand see their social media pages, their messages are cohesive and it will help their audience as a guide.

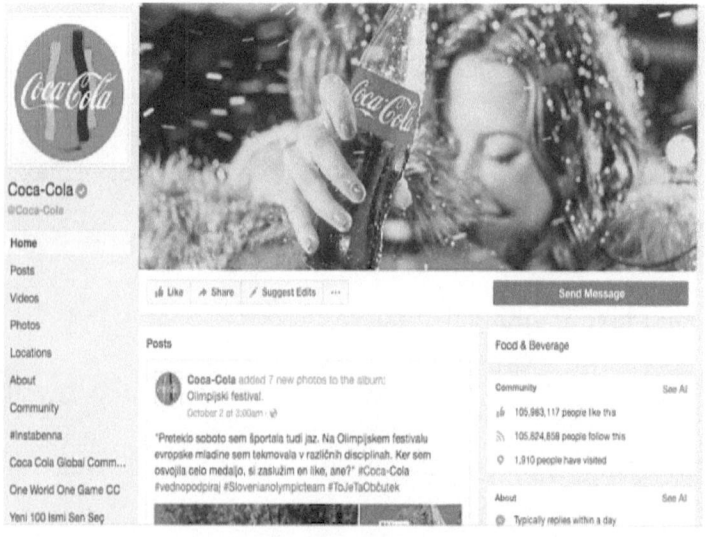

cocacola ✓ **Follow** ▾ ···

634 posts   **2.2m** followers   **582** following

Coca-Cola #ShareaCoke us.coca-cola.com

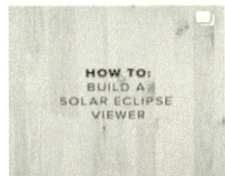  

Tweets	Following	Followers	Likes	Lists
222K	**65.1K**	**3.39M**	**17.4K**	**11**

Follow   ⋮

Coca-Cola ✓
@CocaCola
#ShareaCoke
⌖ Atlanta, GA
⬋ coca-cola.com
🗓 Joined March 2009

Tweets   Tweets & replies   Media

Coca-Cola ✓ @CocaCola · 22h
Must 🍴 Eat 🌮 Taco 🌮 Must. Have. Ice-Cold. Coca-Cola. #NationalTacoDay #ServeWithACoke

Who to follow Refresh · View all

Pepsi™ @pepsi
Follow

McDonald's @McDonalds
Follow

101

Emotion

How can you explain someone spending thousands of dollars to buy a Lamborghini rather than buying some cheaper cars which are equivalent to a Lamborghini, but their heart whispers "Buy a Lambo, buy a Lambo" but do you ever wonder why? It's all because of emotional branding. This type of branding is extremely powerful, they connect with their dream clients emotionally.

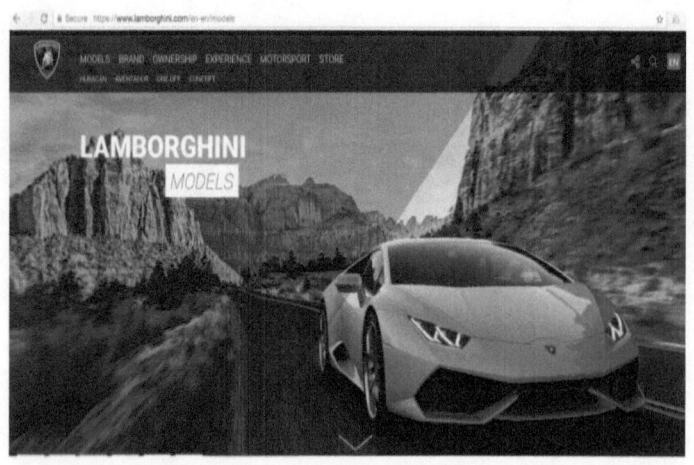

Automobili Lamborghini uses an emotional

branding method around its dream clients by creating a community around its brand. They provide their dream clients an opportunity to feel like they're part of the world's largest Lamborghini community In branding you should develop an easy way to connect with your dream clients on a deeper emotional level, Solve their problems and make them feel like they're the part of the family, Use emotional triggers that acquire your new dream clients and strengthen your existing relationship with your clients.

Flexibility

This is a fast-changing world, to stay relevant and ahead of your competition you should remain flexible.

In my childhood, I liked to use a Nokia

phone (Java powered, non-touch), I was really impressed with the device I used it, especially for gaming purpose. After a couple of years, Android phones were released and I switched my Nokia phone to an Android touch phone. Nokia was not flexible enough to keep with the competition and it was kicked out of the market.

Now you may be thinking, I said you should be consistent, then how can I be flexible by remaining consistent?

Consistency builds standards for your brand, but flexibility will help your brand to build interest and stay ahead of the competition and it allows you to be creative with your marketing campaigns.

As a Marketer, you should focus to create effective identity programs to make your brand identity between your target audience, along with that you should create enough variations to keep your brand fresh as humans and stay ahead of your competitors.

The great example of being flexible is the Old Spice brand they were famous in between old men in earlier days, but eventually, it was almost kicked out of the market by the competitors, but the brand's marketing strategy and flexibility allowed it to regain its position and become a popular brand for men of all ages.

To regain their position in their market, they

teamed up with Wieden and Kennedy and launched new commercials, new websites along new product packings and new product names which helped them to get popular among the younger generations and strengthen their brand.

If your old branding strategies are not working anymore, then don't be afraid to change, it doesn't mean if your old strategies worked in the past will work now, because the world is changing every day. Always try to find new strategies and opportunities to engage with your new audience and remind your existing clients why they love you.

Loyalty

Loyalty is a critical aspect of any brand strategy, If your business already has a good amount of clients and if they love you, then reward them for their love. These customers are your brand ambassadors, they have gone out of their way to write about you, say about you to their friends and to post good reviews about your business on the Internet. Find these clients and reward them, sometimes a Thank You is enough, but you can go beyond that by providing free products or services. You can ask them to write a review about your business online if you have a testimonial section on your website feature them on it.

Cultivating loyalty will help you to increase your brand reputation, increases your recurring conversions and attracts your dream clients toward your business.

Competitive Awareness

In the market, you should aware of your competitors, and be competitive by improving your own strategies and create value in your brand by proving your best products and services to your dream clients. You should watch your competitors closely to know the strategies which they're following? How they're acquiring new clients in your target market? Do some of their baits fail and which ones are succeeding? You can use these pieces of information to tailor your brand to make it better than your competitors.

One of the best examples comes from Oreo, how they saved bowl Sunday.

During the New Orleans Super Bowl of 2013, the stadium experienced an electric outage that postponed the game for 32min and left live viewers bored and irritated, But the Brand prepared themselves with the best 15 social media marketers and they were waiting to respond to any event which took place during the super bowl,

The Oreo's marketing team created a tweet under 5 minutes, which later referred to as "One of the best Super Bowl ads, bar none"

The tweet simply said: "Power out? You can still drink in the dark." It was later raved about by many major news outlets, including the Wall Street Journal and Washington Post. The ad ended up generating more than 16,000 retweets and taking its place in the memory of both sports and marketing fans for the years to come.

Analyzing your competitors' strategies is critical if you like to enhance your brand, but don't allow your competitors to reverse track the moves you make. You may be selling products or services which are similar to your competitor, but you're in business and your brand is unique. By analyzing every move they take don't lose your brand differentiation. [Be Unique]

SECRET #10

Growth Hacking

Many of you might have heard the word "Growth Hacking" some of you might be new to Growth Hacking, Growth hacking is the reason why few numbers of startups manage to achieve high growth rates within a few years. Many of them say growth hacking is dead, but for me, it's not dead, but it does change, what used to work earlier doesn't work anymore.

Examples of growth hacking

The best examples of growth hacking are

Facebook, Airbnb, and Dropbox.

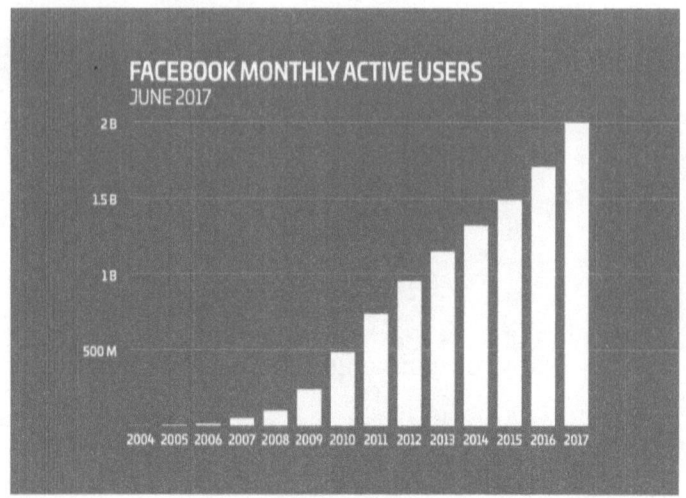

Facebook Growth

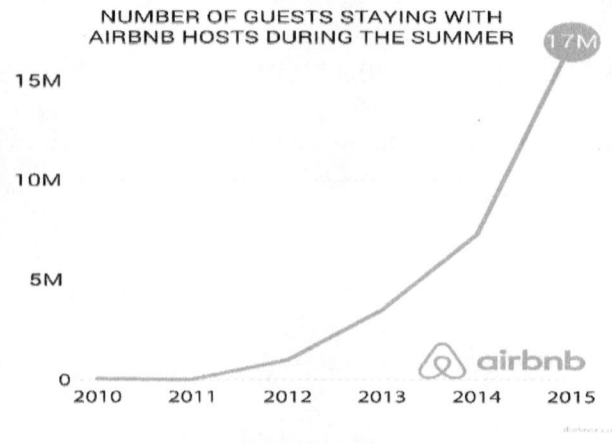

Airbnb Growth

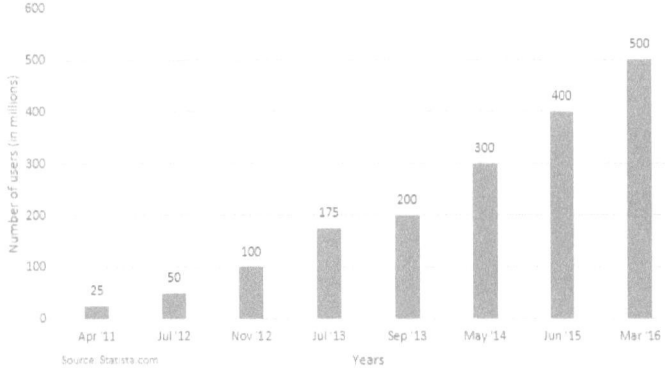

Dropbox Growth

Growth hacking is becoming an important factor for a startup and most of them are looking forward to employing growth hackers, the reason behind to employ growth hackers is to grow faster than their competitors, dominate their markets and generate millions of dollars in revenue.

A growth hacker does not care about budgets, conversions or any other factor, they only focus

113

to grow as fast as they can. [Grow or die], Yeah, I know you need resources to fuel up your startup growth and it's not only money that acts as the fuel, but also the analytical, inexpensive, creative and innovative strategies you use to grow your dream clients.

Remember this truth:

"In this world, you're either growing or you're dying, so get in motion and grow" - Lou Holtz

Now you may be thinking who is a growth hacker? A growth hacker can be anyone in your organization, it can be an engineer, designer or developer. Growth hacking comes when all channels of your organization work together to achieve growth, not just the marketing team it can be the product, engineering or even sales team.

Growth Hacking Strategies to boost your conversions

Partner with other Brands

Partnerships are the best way to hunt your dream clients organically, reach out to other brands to partner with your business so that both of you get the benefit if you already have 90,000 clients and the other brand have 110,000 clients you both can work together to reach 200,000 clients. I'm not asking you to partner with your competitors, instead, find the right business which compliments your business.

For example, see Red Bull & GoPro

GoPro sells cameras while Red Bull sells energy drinks. They're both lifestyle brands with similar goals

They have lots of things in common and some of them are:

- Action-packed
- Adventurous
- Fearless
- Extreme

These make them a perfect pair for marketing campaigns (mostly in action sports) GoPro provides the best tools for athletes to capture their stunts, races, and events. In turn, Red Bull puts and sponsors the events.

These companies had done several campaigns together and one of the notable campaigns was "Stratos". In this campaign Felix Baumgartner had a GoPro on his hand and jumped from a space pod above 24 miles of the Earth, he set 3 world records but also showed the potential humans that define Red Bull and GoPro.

Of course I know, you're not GoPro or Red Bull to conduct big events, but that doesn't mean you can't do it, you can always find innovative ways to hunt your clients in organic ways, Like tagging each other on Social meads, cross-posting or promoting each other on your websites or You can even offer product bundles.

Establish your Social presence

If you're competing with huge players in the market, you might not able to dominate most popular platforms like Facebook or Twitter, but you can find the social platforms which your competitors are not using and build your audience over there, once you had dominated that social platform your competitors will struggle to build their audience in that social network where your business is well established.

Once your business is established in all social platforms you can use it to send organic traffic to your website and vice versa.

Give away something for free

The giveaway is the fastest way to get more people interested in your brand,

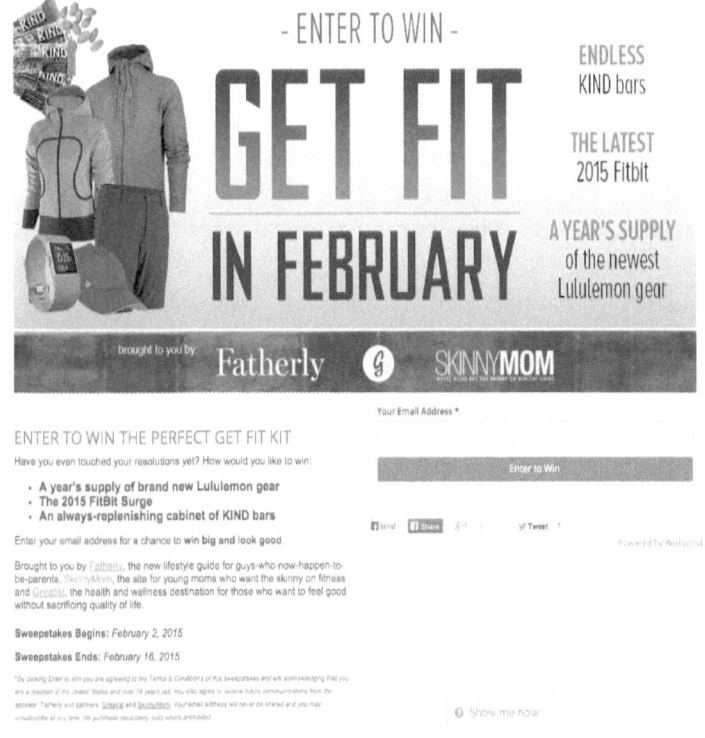

A Social media giveaway campaign can be

effective when you hype it in many places as much as you can to gather participation and you can also reward peoples to share and spread your campaign to their friends. You can also give away something special when a customer buys your product or services.

The above image shows a Facebook giveaway campaign that collected 49,000 emails, 57,100 views, and 85.94% conversion rate for prizes worth $1200. You may be wondering why this giveaway campaign was successful?

Teaming up with other brands: Fatherly the one who ran the Facebook campaign teamed up with Greatest and Skinny Mom and they agreed to split the leads and promote together.

Asking for email: This is the information which the merchants aimed to collect when they conducted the campaign, this played a major role in the conversion part as you can see the campaign had more than 85% conversions. If you're asking for more information most of the people who visit the campaign won't fill up the fields so make it simple most of the people are lazy nowadays.

The Prize: Prizes are a great way to increase the chance of someone entering your giveaway campaign and providing the details you're asking for.

The perfect time: The best time to run a fitness-related campaign in February. People haven't yet given up on their New Year's resolution and a price pack of athletic wear and health bars is a great offer, exactly what people are thinking about in February.

Conduct consistent A/B testing

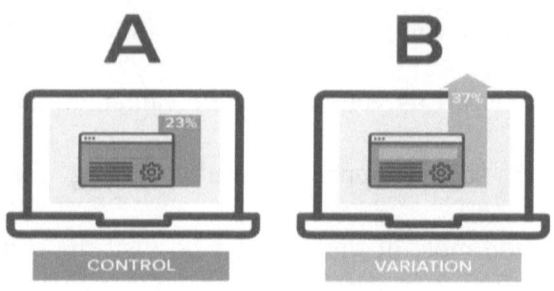

A/B testing is an important factor in Growth Hacking you have to consistently check how your funnels are converting. If something is not working you have to test it against a variation to know why your funnels are not working. I recommend conducting an A/B testing for every part of your website like:

- **Homepage**
- **Landing page**
- **Ends of Blog posts**
- **Sales pages**
- **Contact page**
- **About Us page**

Focus on one area of each page and make small changes so you can understand what impacted your outcome otherwise you're going to skew your conversion results.

Use tools like Crazy Egg to set up A/B tests on your website this can provide you with lots of pieces of information and reports of user behaviors on your website so that you can conduct more effective A/B testing.

Design for conventions

If your Landing page sucks then no one is going to show an interest in your business so make sure your website is well optimized for conversion make sure to conduct a website load time test and to conduct tests to make sure your website is mobile-friendly. If you don't have great visuals and don't excite your audience, then maybe it's time to go back to your whiteboard to make a new design (Look does matter).

If you had already done A/B testing and you're still getting low conversions, then you have to look into your website design and ask yourself "What would convince yourself to convert if you're a customer?"

NOTE: If you're using a CDN (Content delivery network) to increase website loading speed, then make sure to visit your website from different locations through your web browser by using a VPN (Virtual Private Network) so that you can make sure in all countries your website is loading correctly, In my carrier I had seen a lot of websites which works properly in their country but when the same website is visited from a different country we can see it as a broken website. So, make sure your website is working properly in all countries.

Engage Your Audience with emails

I had done this sever times throughout my business and it was a huge success, Email is still a powerful medium of communication, I occasionally send out an email to my subscriber list to email me back by asking questions, suggestions, comments, etc. In this way, I build a bold relationship with my clients.

One of the worst things I see nowadays is DONOTREPLAY (donotreplay@example.com) emails, this only means you're not interested in what your clients have to say. These emails close the communication between your client and your business and it will break the bond between you two, By opening the communication you can see a lot of conversion changes and you will receive a lot of useful pieces of information from your audience.

Go offline

A true growth hacker will always find innovative ways to reach the ultimate goal "GROWTH", this includes going offline.

If there are events going on in different areas, then participate in them reserve a booth for your business and use it to establish new relationships with your dream clients and businesses, nothing beats a business which goes offline because meeting peoples face to face, shaking their hands will make your business more attractive and you will stand out of the competition.

Create content which goes viral

The best way to market your business is by word of mouth and viral content like a viral explainer video will be enough to promote your product and bring a huge amount of traffic to your website.

Look forward to creating a hilarious explainer video which put your product or services in light, this had worked for dozens of startups it will work you too.

One of the best examples is: Poo-Pourri's product explainer video that went viral

This video was so clever that it ended up creating 40 Million views, made their brand popular along with that it helped them to dominate a huge market share.

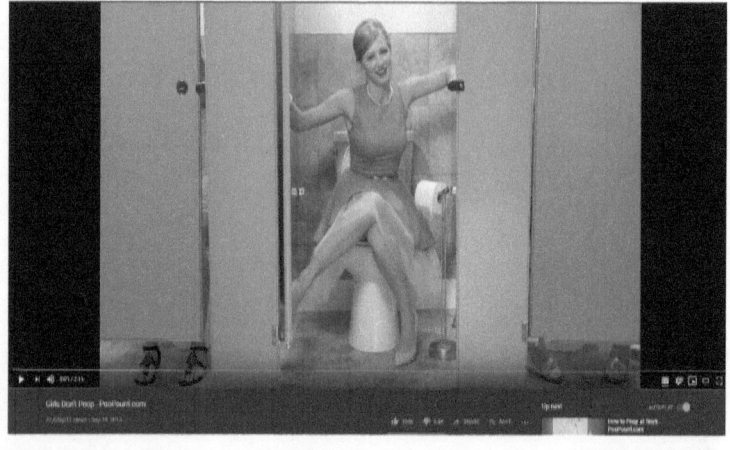

The video was so powerful that peoples

recommended it to others by word of mouth.

Offer a freemium option

If you're running a Software as a Service (SaaS) company then you need to consider developing a freemium business model, it works great for all likes of apps, Offer something for free and convince your dream clients to switch to the paid version of your software, it's the best way to get people in the first step of Value Ladder.

I know most of the users in the initial stage won't convert into paying clients, but in the long run, it will give you lots of benefits. Once they start to get benefit from your software, they'll want more of it and slowly they will change to paid customers.

"Market a business such a way that, people

crave for your services like drugs."

Freemium model helps you to get new clients faster on the value ladder so it works well and you can use these clients to make a recurring income than acquiring new clients.

SECRET #11

Spy on your Competitors

Nowadays spying on your competitors is very critical, if you want to dominate the market, You need to look into your competitors to know what they're doing, what's working for them, what's not working for them and try to implement the same strategies which worked for them to your business it will boost your chances to succeed and save a lot of money in the long run.

Learn from your competitors and hear what your clients have to say about your business and you will succeed"

Remember this Truth:

"If you want to be successful, find someone who has achieved the results you want and copy what they do and you'll achieve the same results." - Tony Robbins

What we're going to do here is to identify who are your competitors, what are their strengths and weaknesses and what strategies are they using.

Those who are reading this book, who are new to the marketing world might be thinking now we're doing something illegal, but the fact is we're not doing anything illegal, it's an acceptable practice of discovering new opportunities.

Spying on your competitors can save you a lot of time in the long run and you can use these data which you collected to discover new opportunities, differentiate yourself, learn from the competitors' mistakes, Dominate the market and most importantly to stay alert in your industry.

It's time to dig deeper…

Identify your competitors

You may have a lot of competitors in the market with different organization sizes, all of them fall under two categories.

Direct Competitors

These are the organizations that are directly competing with you to hunt your dream clients.

Indirect Competitors

These are the organizations which offer similar products or services as you do for your dream clients, but they may be selling these products or services from different locations or to a specific demographics these organizations can be from different industries, list them out and collect the data off them so that it will help you in the long run and opens new opportunities for your business.

There are many techniques which we can use to identify our competitors.

The competitors you already know

If you are going to start your business or maybe you had started one, you may come across some of your competitors who target your clients. If you do know about some of your competitors, then it's a good start writing their names on your whiteboard. The chances are you will write down a couple of names that pop up in your mind, but it's not enough for our analysis so we should use other techniques to find the remains competitors.

Search for your competitors in various search engines

Use almost all search engines you know, like Google, Bing, Yahoo, etc.. To find your direct competitors.

Search the relevant keywords for your business in search engines and see what they come up with as search results.

Once you go through the search results you will notice some search ads (PPC) and the websites ranking organically (SEO) for that keyword, either way, all these peoples are looking forward to hunting your dream clients.

For Example, your business is selling jewelry online then you can search in the search box like "Engagement ring Toronto" and in the search results, you can see the direct competitors now add their names in your competitors' lists.

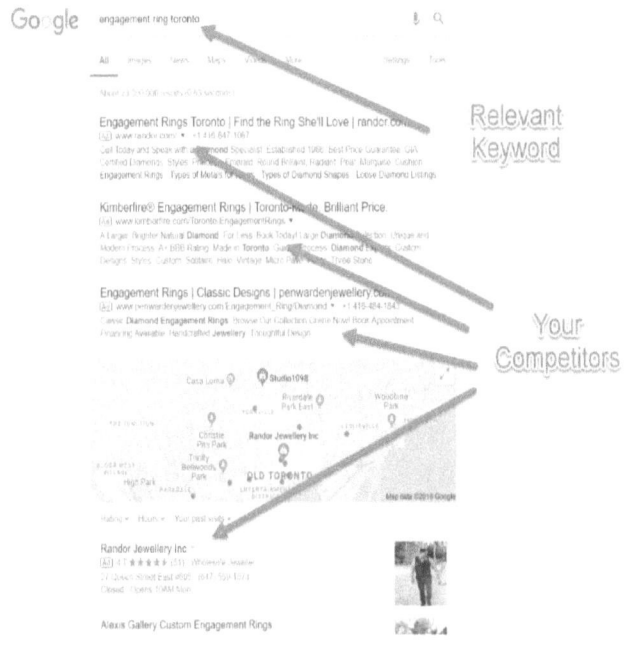

If you're not getting ideas of what keywords to search in search engines, then you can use tools like **Ubersuggest** and **Answer the Public** to generate keywords for your business.

Using Google Search Operators

Google search operators are symbols that can be included in your search queries to get more useful pieces of information.

There are lots of search operators some of them are

- $ symbol (For Example: "bags $100")
- @ symbol (For Example @twitter) mainly used to fetch social media results
- To get the exact results which match your keyword, then use "[keyword]"

To find our competitors, we will use the term **related:** in front of your own web address and Google to fetch out the results which are similar to your business.

For Example: If you're searching for the competitors of amazon then type **related:amazon.com** and google will list their competitors in the search results.

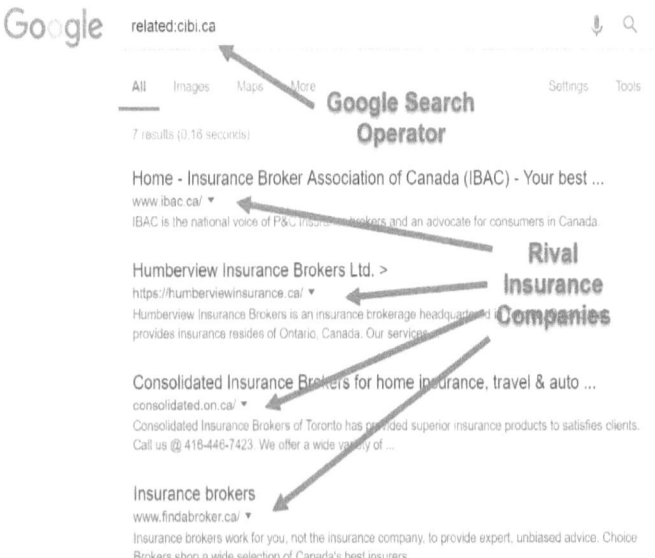

Identify your competitors using SpyFu

Spy Fu is a spying tool that helps you to gather competitive intelligence and identify your organic and paid competitors.

You can type your website URL into their search box and you will get a good number of pieces of information about you as well as your competitors, by using this tool you can also find the competitors of your competitors.

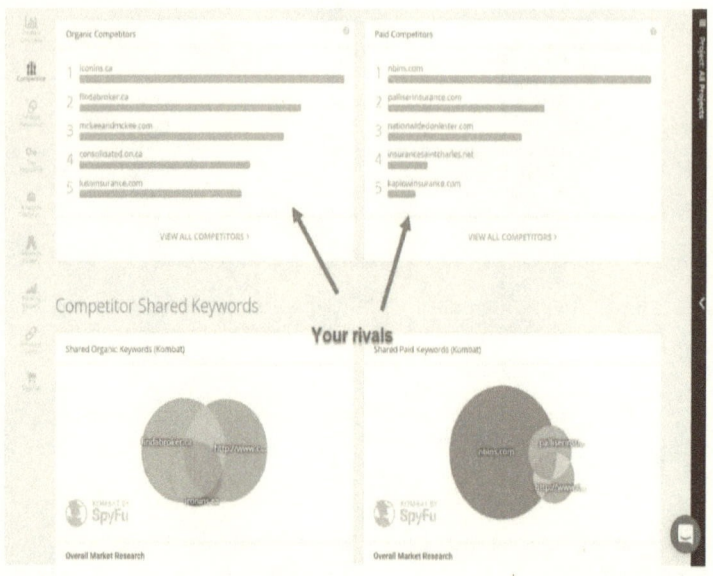

This is the best tool to analyze your competitors, Pay Per Click (PPC) and Search Engine Optimization (SEO) competitive analysis and backlink research.

Discover using Similar Web

This is one of the top tools for competitive research and analysis. It can help you to identify your competitors and similar websites like yours. You can enter your website URL and find out the companies which are hunting your dream clients.

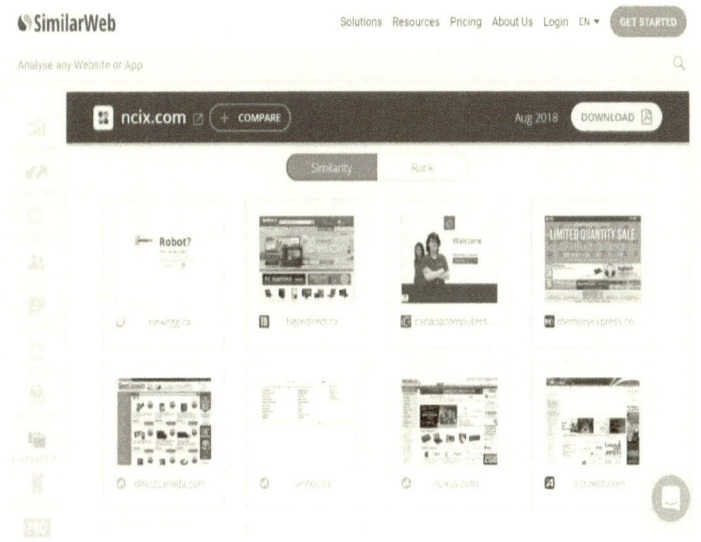

You can enter your competitors' URL into this tool and you can find out which websites are referring them, backlinks, where they are running their ads, what are their successful Ad campaign, who are their audiences, traffic and a lot more.

Similar Web is an All in One tool that can do more than identifying your competitors I highly recommend to check this tool.

Find your competitors using Google Maps

Google Maps is the best option to find out Local Businesses that are competing with you. To do that you can use some keywords such as "**[type of business] near me**" or "**[type of business] in [location]**"

For Example, if you're running an Apple service center, then you can search for "**apple service center near New York**" to see the list of your competitors in New York.

Using Google Maps, you can find out your Local Competitors as well as you will get some idea to improve your Search Engine Optimization (SEO).

Use Local Directories to find your competitors

Local industry directories consist of useful pieces of information about your competitors in your area that are hunting for your dream clients, you can use local directories and review websites like the Yellow Pages, Found Locally, Foursquare, Yelp and lot more to find them.

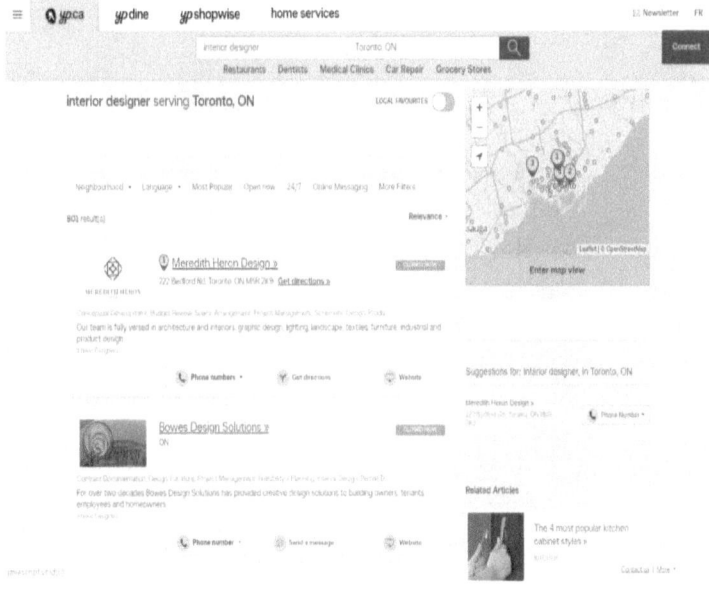

Conducting competitor research through local directories will help you a lot if you're working as a small business or in a local market.

Analyze your competitors

Once you had collected the list of your competitors, then it's time to analyze them, there are several ways to analyze your competitors.

Examine your competitor websites and its UX design

When it comes to analyzing your competitors, it is better to start with visiting and analyzing their websites and see how they had created their websites for conversions. While observing the competitor's website make sure you inspect the following elements:

- Check the overall website design and elements of the website.
- Check how their landing page and home page looks like in Mobile and Desktop, How and where they had included social proofs, trust marks, symbols, and logos.
- Check their call to action (CTA) buttons and

analyze what types of colors and fonts they're using to stand out and see is it will encourage new clients to click through.

- The pages they included in Header and Footer sections on their website.

Car Insurance in Toronto, Ontario

- Check which social channels are linked to their website.
- Check out the images they're using and see it's good enough to encourage a new client to stay on the website for a long time.
- See how they're collecting emails and analyze the login, sign up, popup and contact forms of

their website.

- See there is live chat assistance on the website.

If your competitors are eCommerce related then it's crucial to check the following:

- The type of products they sell, what type of photos are they are used in their products, is it compelling enough?

- Check the zooming effects of the products they're selling.

- Read their product descriptions, reviews, and other pieces of information available on the product detail page.

- See what type of product ratings they follow. (Stars, numbers or anything else).

- Analyze their Add to Cart button and buy now buttons and see where they're placed and what color they use.

- If they're selling variable products see how and where they placed the product variation buttons and size chat button.

- Check they use breadcrumbs on their website for easy navigation and SEO.

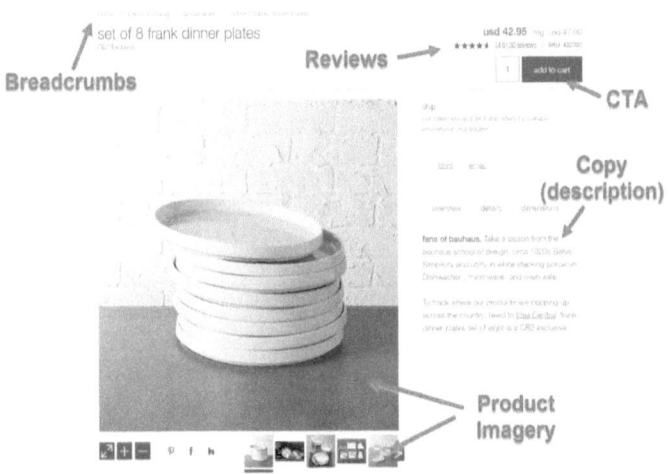

Check their websites to see what type of conversion optimization strategies they're using; see they're following urgency and scarcity models.

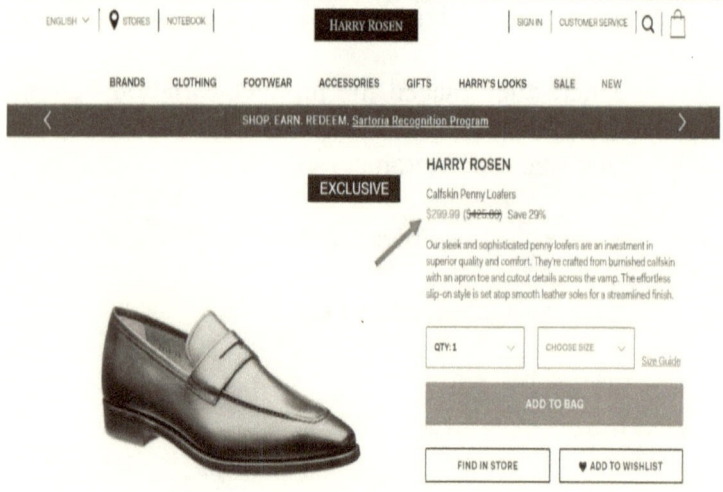

After checking the virtual inception of the website, now you have to check how fast their website is loaded? Is their website optimized for mobile devices? And which technologies they used to develop their website? You can use **Page Speed Insights** and **Mobile Friend Test** tools by Google to conduct these tests.

Each website is different but you can use the insights which you collected from your competitors' websites to design and find new optimization opportunities to increase the conversion rate of your website.

Find the traffic sources of your competitors

One of the important factors in spying your competitors is analyzing your competitors' traffic.

You need to reverse hack their strategies to know more about their traffic, from which locations do they come from? Which devices are they using? What are their main traffic sources: it paid, referral, social, organic or direct?

Once you analyze your competitors' traffic, you will get an extreme idea about where your dream clients reside on the Internet and which type of traffic you need to invest in most.

You can use tools like **SEM Rush** to investigate the sources of your competitors' web traffic. You have to type in your competitor's URL on SEM Rush and it will analyze and generate a report similar to this:

With SEM Rush you will get more insights into your competitors' Bounce Rates, Number of Visits, Unique Visitors, Pages per visit, average visit duration and lot more.

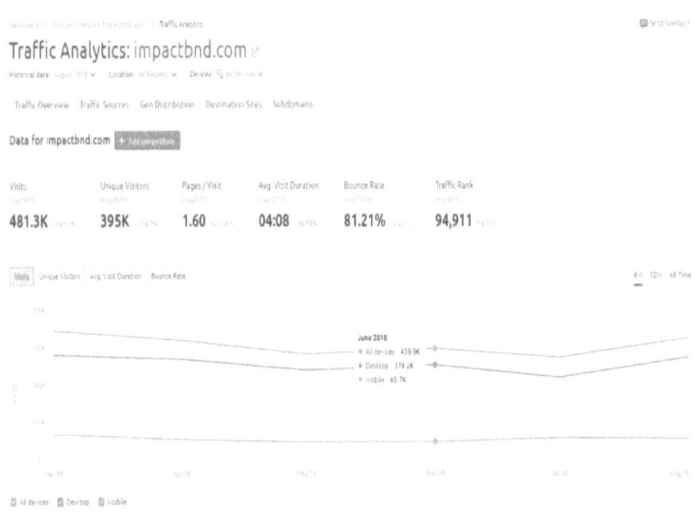

This tool will help you to gather all pieces of information about your competitors' web traffic strategies, Before SEM Rush these pieces of information were only available in your competitors' Google Analytics accounts now with the help of SEM Rush you can have these pieces of information at your fingertips.

Inspect your competitors' content

If you're in the marketing field, then you might come across the truth "Content is King" since it's the backbone of digital marketing. Great content can rank you higher in Google and other search engines along with that it educates your web traffic to learn and interact with your business. Content plays an important role in selling your products and services to your dream clients so it's great if you spend some time analyzing your competitors' contents.

Make a note about the following factors in your competitors' website:

- What type of content they publish, is it a video, blog post, podcasts, eBook, webinars, etc.?
- Is there a blog section on their website?
- How many contents do they publish in a week?
- Determine the quality of their content.
- What are their interesting topics?
- See how many peoples engage in their blogs?

(Like commenting, linking, sharing, etc.)

To get notified when someone publishes a new post on the internet related to your target audience or your target keywords, then it's better you start using **Google Alert** and you can also use Google Alert to notify you whenever someone mentions your business or your competitors in any newly published posts.

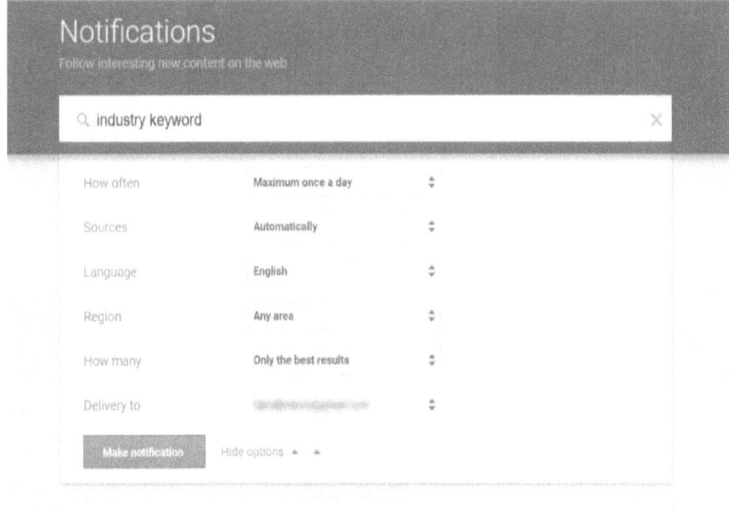

One of the great tools available in the market to spy on trending topics and high performing posts is **BuzzSumo.** You can use this tool to gather more pieces of information about high performing contents and it will help you to collect answers to some mysterious questions like, what's making their contents to perform well? And how you can use these pieces of information to get the same results in your business?

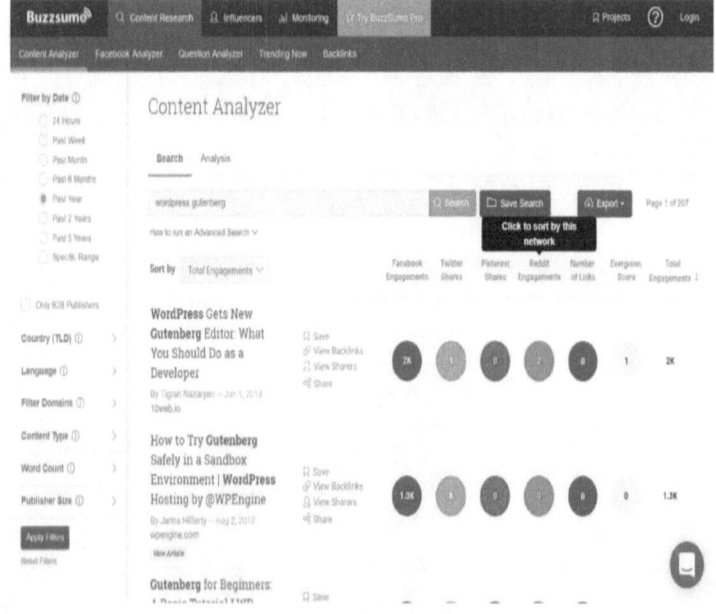

Last but not least, subscribe to your competitors' newsletters to keep you updated about their business and their contents, it will also help you to reverse hack their email marketing strategies.

Analyze competitors' Search Engine Optimization

Search Engine Optimization is an important factor when it comes to ranking in various search engines like Google, Bing, etc. If you do it right, you will start to see a huge amount of organic traffic on your website.

To rank properly in search engines, you need to use your target keyword correctly in the following places:

- The Image Titles.
- The URL Architecture.

- H1 Tags.
- Internal Links and Image ALT Text
- Contents

If you like to dig deeper into your competitors' target keywords than you can use tools like **Ahref Site Explorer** for that.

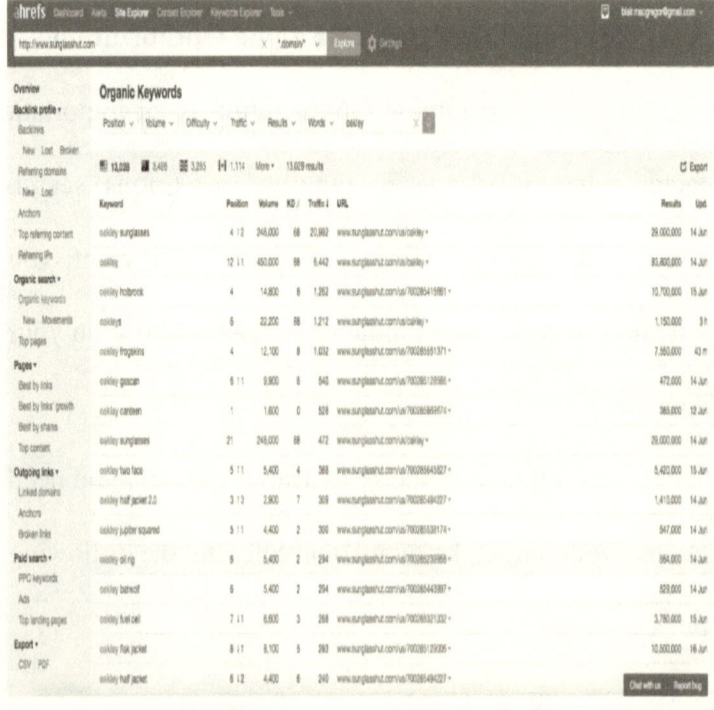

With the help of Ahref Site Explorer, you

can know the position of your competitor in Search Engine Results Page (SERP), their number of unique visitors, list of target keywords that your competitors are ranking for and other valuable pieces of information.

You can use SEM Rush to collect SEO pieces of information from your competitors, but the pieces of information are limited as compared to Ahref Site Explorer.

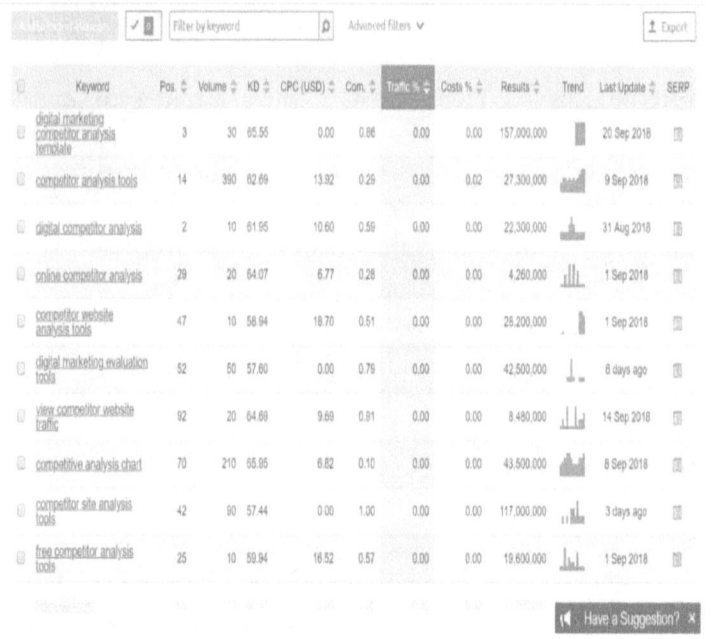

Analyze your Rivals backlink sources

Backlinks are one of the important factors which search engines like Google uses to determine your rank on their Search Engine Results Page (SERP), The higher your score in SERP the higher you rank in search engines and they consider your website as the trustworthy source of information. As a marketer or a small business owner, it's important to build as many backlinks as possible for your website. Backlink building is time-consuming and it takes a lot of patience and effort to succeed in the long run. Knowing your competitors' backlink structures will help you to construct your own highly effective backlink structure for your business.

You can use tools like Moz Open Site Explorer and SEM Rush to spy on your competitors' backlinks.

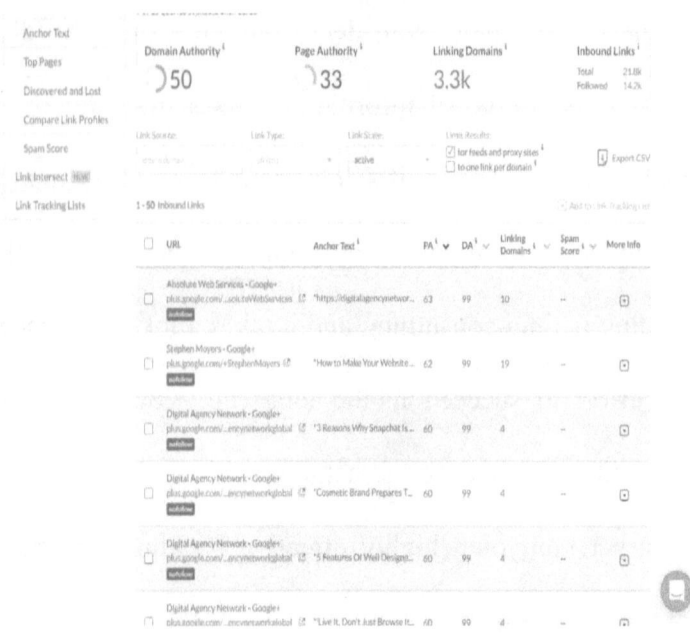

SEM Rush will help you to dig deeper into backlink analysis by generating reports like these:

Data for digitalagencynetwork.com   + Add competitors

Advertising & Marketing · Business Operations   Show all 3

Total Backlinks	Referring Domains	Referring IPs	Authority Score
69.4K	737	873	53

New & Lost Backlinks

Chart Scope: Root Domain   ☑ New ☑ Lost ◆ Score ▾

Aug 20, 2018
● New 5,509
◆ Lost 1,019

Total Backlinks

Chart Scope: Root Domain   ◆ Score ▾

Backlink Types

98%	1%		<1%
68.7K text	713 image	form	2 frame

Follow vs Nofollow

7%   **93%**

5K Follow   68.7K nofollow

TLD Distribution

TLD	Domain (N)	TLD	Domain (N)
.gov	8	.uk	
.edu	2	.co	
.com	424	.de	
.org	40	.info	
.net	3	other	

View full report

Country

Country	Domain (N)
United States of America	417
Germany	12
United Kingdom	17
France	3
Netherlands	23

View full report

Top Anchors

digitalagency	49,276
dacia conger	4,356
vivian hilder	4,344
https://digitalagenc...m/ag...	3,216
https://digitalagenc...ag...	2,416

Top Anchor Terms

digitalagency	49,276
hilder	4,356
dacia	4,356
vivian	4,344
conger	

Make your pricing model competitive and analyze their shipping and return policies

Pricing of your products or services is very critical, A competitive pricing model will help you to sell more products and services more effectively, Nowadays, most of the customers compare prices of products and services from different businesses and picks the right one for them, so it's an important factor to make your pricing more competitive.

Analyzing your competitors' pricing models will help you to know how much your dream clients are willing to pay for your products and services which solves their problem.

Shipping and return policies are important factors of an e-commerce business because 66% of online shoppers abound shopping carts because of high shipping costs and bad return policies. If you're noticing cart abandonments in your eCommerce business, then reach out to them and find out the reason behind their cart abandonments and give a hand (offers, coupons or deals) and bring them abroad, It's always better to call them personally than emailing them and send automated personal emails when any new client purchases your products or services.

If you can offer a free shipping and 30 day return policy, then it's going to be great, yeah, I know this is not a perfect world and most of the new businesses can't provide free shipping, if that's the case, then you should check your competitors shipping costs and return policies and make changes to your shipping costs and return policies more competitive.

Use the Reviews

Analyze the reviews of your competitors including everything from products or services reviews on their website to social media reviews and comments on their blog.

If your competitors are local businesses then you can use google search results to see the ratings and reviews.

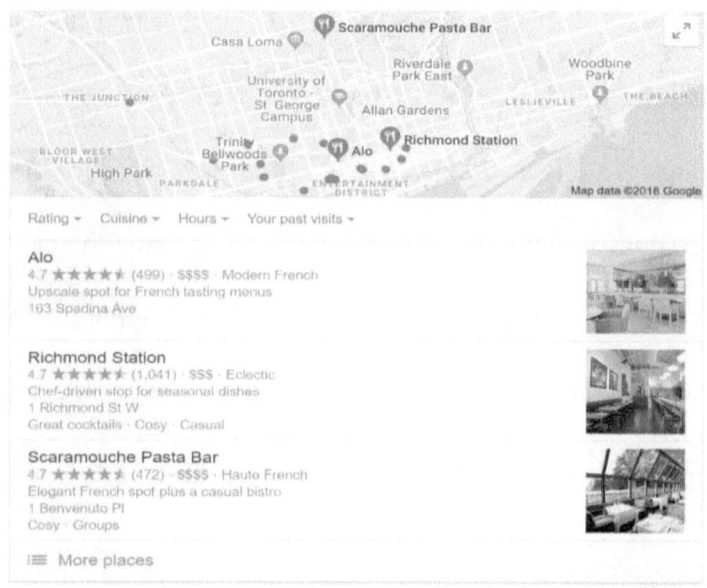

Analyzing reviews about your competitors will help you to gather more insights about your competitors' strengths and weaknesses and the weaknesses are the golden eggs you can use them to improve your products or services. Make sure to look into each comment of the reviewers and list out what they're complaining about making sure to keep close attention on 1 to 3-star reviews because they might contain the most useful pieces of information. Use these pieces of information to improve your business and stand out from the competition. If you found lots of reviews in any products or services similar to yours, then well, congratulations it simply means people are interested in buying your products or services.

Monitor your competitors' social media

Social media are an important factor in online business since it helps to interact with your audience and helps to establish a relationship and build a brand over it.

Analyze your competitors' social media to learn how's they're using social networks to influence their audience.

Conduct an audit of your competitors' social media pages:

- Check out their profile pictures and cover photos. Is it memorable or helps to easily recognize their brand?
- Read your competitors' bio.
- See what type of content they're posing? Are they following engaging with their content?
- How frequently they're posted on their page?
- How many followers do they have? And who are they?

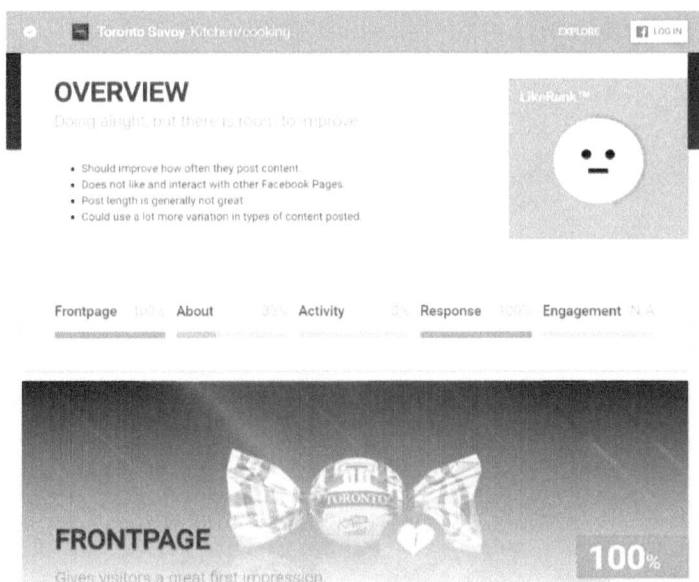

Use tools like **Likealyzer** to conduct full audit tests. Find out all pages of your competitors on different social platforms and conduct full audit tests for each of them. If your competitors have a huge number of followers then it simply means you have a huge market out there for your products and services.

Hack your competitors' email marketing funnels

Email marketing is one of the important strategies is a business, it helps to drive organic traffic to your website and buy your products and services again and again. Effective Email campaigns are crucial in business if any of your competitors has an effective email campaign than yours, then you can reverse hack their email marketing funnel to upgrade it and implement it on your business.

To reverse hack your competitors' email marketing funnels first you have to navigate to their website and sign up for their News Letter and other services and wait for their upcoming emails.

Make sure you track these factors:

- When you receive your competitors' marketing emails? And how frequently you receive them?

- Analyze the content and visuals of their emails, and what kind of message are they sent to their clients?

- Analyze the emails to find out if they're offering any kind of discounts, coupons, or deals through their emails

- Are they using scarcity and urgency strategy on their emails like countdown timers, coupon expires timers, social proofs, etc.

- Analyze their Call to Action (CTA) buttons.

- Most importantly, see the Subject Line, which they use to make their clients open their emails.

You can also buy some products or services from your competitors to receive their Upsell offers and you can model them in your business. If you're running an eCommerce business, then make sure to add some products in the cart of your competitors' website and wait to receive the cart abandonment emails.

You can use **Click Bank** an affiliate marketplace to create your email marketing campaign.

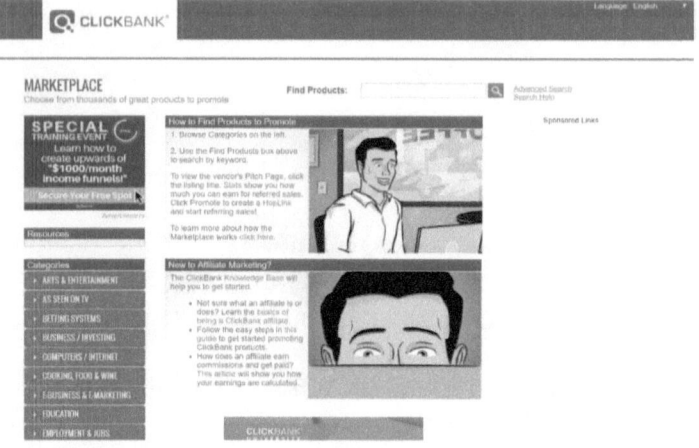

Head over to click bank website and find a category which represents your industry, then look for products or services which is similar to yours and when you find them, click on the affiliate page, It will show you the best instructions to set up an email campaign which is specially designed to sell those products and services.

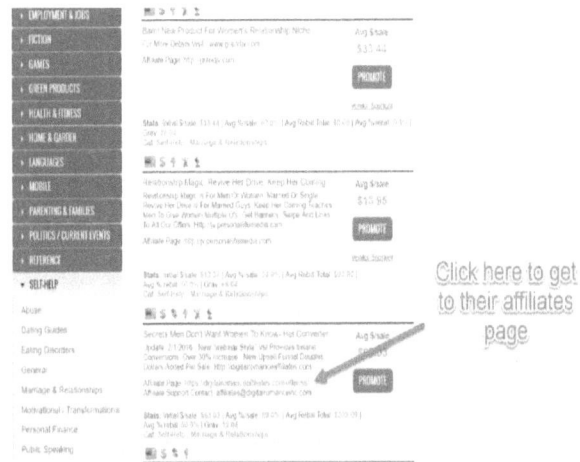

These instructions are proven to work so implement it on your website and see how your clients convert into paying clients.

Monitor Mentions

Use **Social Mentions**, a tool which helps you to monitor what peoples are saying about your business, your competitors on blogs and other social networks. You can use this tool to dig out how many times your target keywords were mentioned in other platforms, You can also subscribe to their RSS feeds or email alerts so that you will be updated frequently. Staying on top of social mentions is the best way to increase your business reputation.

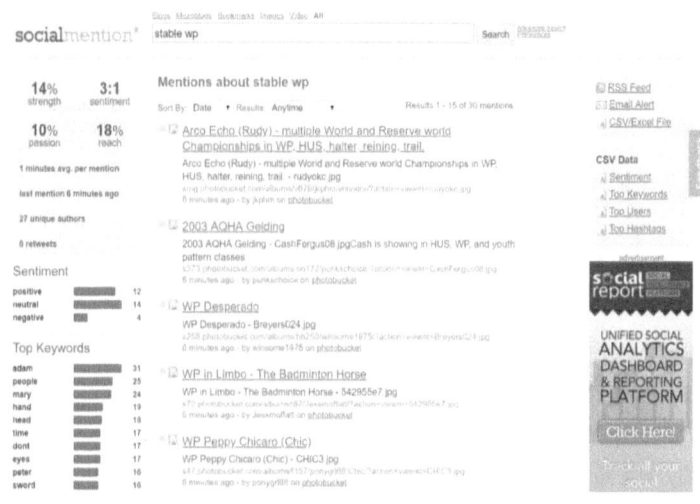

Research Your Competitors Ads.

Running ads is the best way to bring paid traffic to your website from other platforms, since it's paid traffic it's going to cost you money, So make sure you're not wasting money by not targeting your right audiences. If you target your right audiences with proper Ads then your campaign will make you money Return of Investment (ROI).

Google Ads and Facebook Ads are the biggest and best Ad platforms on the Internet and both work in different ways Google helps you to target a specific audience with target keywords and Facebook ads help you to target users by using their Interests, behavior and other data.

If you're a small business and you're thinking to start a paid advertising campaign then it's better to analyze and study the successful Ad campaigns of your competitors and try to create a similar campaign to get similar results.

You can use Spy Fu to find and analyze your competitors' best performing and successful Google Ad campaigns and it helps you to find out profitable keywords to target in your Google Ad campaign.

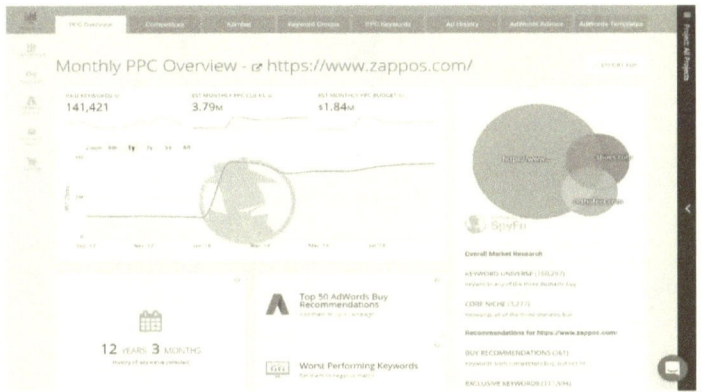

You can use SEM Rush for a similar purpose by using these spying tools you can dig deeper into your competitors display Ad campaigns and Pay Per Click (PPC) campaigns.

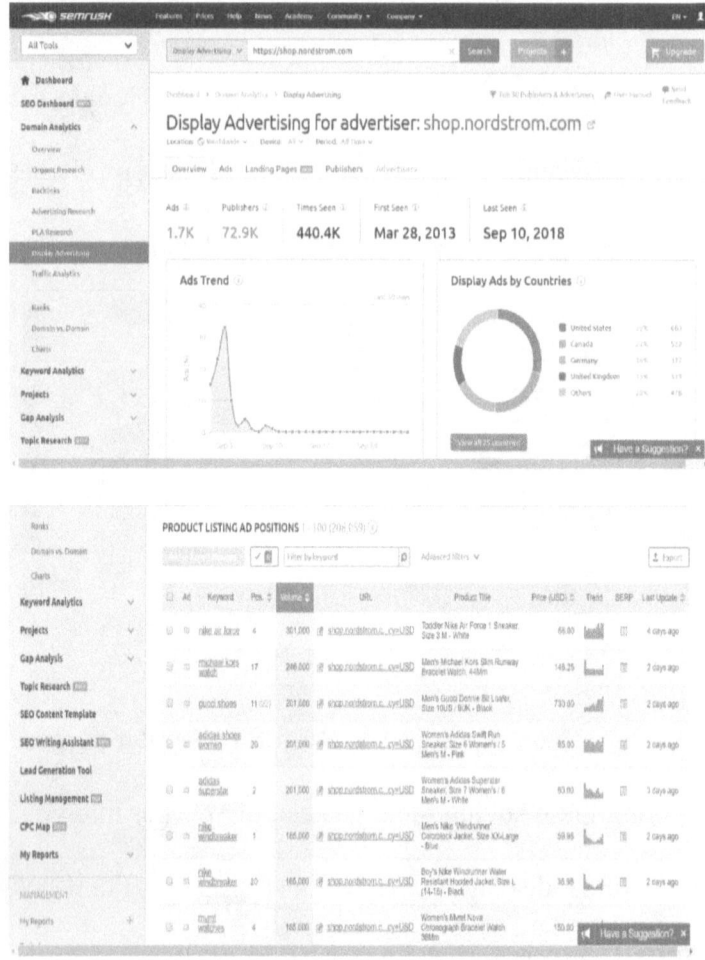

If you're planning to run a Facebook Ad campaign then it's better to use the **AdEspresso** tool which helps you to research and analyze your competitors' Ads which performs well and it also helps you to run best-split tests more effectively. Analyze the top-performing Ads of your competitors using AdEspresso and find out what made them so successful and use those strategies to build your Ad and your Ad campaign and get similar results.

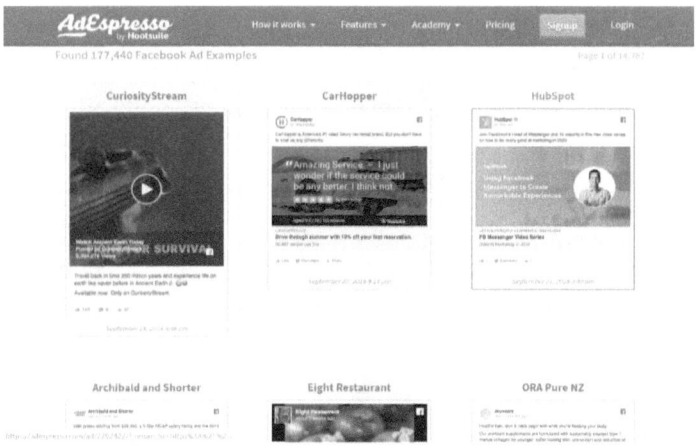

Most of the small business owners forget to use the tool which Facebook provides (**Facebook Insights**) to learn more about their target audience, use it to improve your ad campaign targeting.

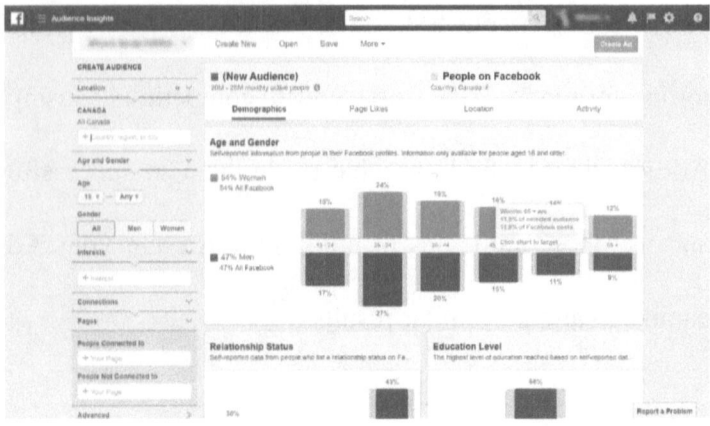

Spying your competitors is vital to learn from your competitors' success and mistakes it will help you to explore more opportunities, save money, time and efforts. Spy on your competitors and keep you updated about your competitors' marketing strategies to stay one step ahead of the competition.

Ubercircle – All in one social Media Management Tool

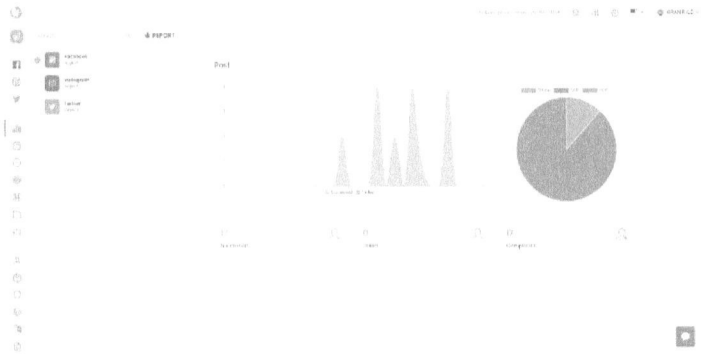

Use tools like Ubercircle
(https://www.kiranrkg.com/ubercircle/) to manage and
automate your social media profiles. It helps you to
schedule, Analyze and automate your social profiles. By
using a social media management tool. You can save a
lot of time, energy and engage with social media
audience.

SECRET #12

Funnel Hacking

After reading the last chapter you might be thinking is there is a way to build a marketing funnel easily? Or is there a way to hack your competitors' marketing funnels? Then funnel hacking is the best way to do it, you can reverse hack your competitors' successful marketing funnels to build your own. It's one of the best strategies for a head start than building an entire marketing funnel from scratch. You should look at your competitors Home pages, Landing pages, sales pages, price, points, emails, retargeting ads, to reverse hack their sales funnel.

List out your best competitors

In the previous chapter, we had discussed different ways to find your competitors. You can also use Facebook and other social media platforms to find your rivals you can see some ads similar to your products and services in your social media news feeds since you might fall in your competitors Facebook advertising demographic.

Analyze your competitors' funnels

In chapter #3 we had discussed what is a marketing funnel, now it's time to recap it. A marketing funnel or a sales funnel is a process which is used by business to bring their dream clients from 'Awareness" to "Purchase."

To reverse hack your competitors' sales funnel you first need to head towards your competitors' website, opt-in copy, email funnels and screenshot everything. Most of you might be thinking why we're taking screenshots? The answer is to get a clear picture of the marketing strategies which is used by your competitors to sell products to their clients. Take the screenshots and save it in a clearly labeled folder on your personal computer.

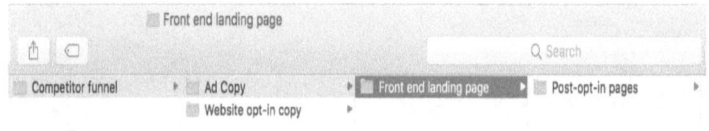

In the above image, I had created directories

within 'competitor funnel' that will hold the directory 'Ad copy' and so on. By following this way, you will get a step by step idea about how your competitors are selling their products and services to your clients.

Funnels can become complicated in different levels the main contents which you need to focus on being:

- **Front end Landing pages:** These are the landing pages that open up when you click an Ad on your competitors.
- **Back end Landing pages:** These are the landing pages that offer up-sells, cross-sells, etc.
- **Ads:** Analyze your competitors' ads to find out what makes them more inspiring and encouraging to bring traffic from other channels to your competitors' landing page.
- **Follow up emails:** Analyze the emails which are sent by your competitors to bring traffic to their website again and again.

Analyze your competitors' sales triggers

When you're going through your competitors' sales funnel, make sure to note down their sales triggers like:

- Catchphrases or common marketing words
- Analyze how they frame their subject lines, headlines, etc.
- Find out their social proofs (can be videos, audio, pictures or written)
- See they're offering anything special like eBook, free webinar or educational videos, etc.
- How many steps did they use to complete a sales funnel?
- Email follow up sequence
- Check prices on their products and services
- Analyze the content and length of your competitors' landing or sales page.

You can use some tools to reverse hack your competitors' sales funnels to build your profitable funnel.

Ghostery

Ghostery is a chrome extension that helps you to find what type of pixels and trackers are placed on your competitors' web pages. That simply means you can see if your competitor has a Facebook pixel, Google remarking tag or any other tracker on their website.

Ghostery helps you to hide from these type of trackers and pixels and it's also the best tool to find out which trackers are used in a website

BuiltWith Technology Profiler

BuiltWith Technology Profiler is a chrome extension that helps you to find out which technologies your competitors used to build their website. It shows you all types of pieces of information like Programming languages used, which Content Management System (CMS) used, Content Delivery Network (CDN) and a lot more.

AdBeat

AdBeat is a powerful tool which can be used to find out the strategies which your competitors are using in the market and how they're spending money on a marketing campaign, the landing pages which their ads lead to, how they're collecting emails and how they're selling their products or services. AdBeat helps you to find what's working for your competitors and it also helps you to implement it on your business.

Use Funnel Hacking as a growth hacking strategy

Your competitors might have many products at various points of their funnels. Your competitors might have different funnels which are hidden, to unlock the mystery goes a step further and purchase all products and services of your competitors and take note of their offers, up-sells, cross-sells, down-sells, etc.

With the pieces of information, you collected from the above tools and the other tools which are introduced in this book you can easily replicate your competitors' sales funnel in your business.

Let's see a successful funnel of a company called Mentor Box which is run by its founder Alex Mehr. Mentor Box is a platform where you can find the summarized video lessons of best-selling books and the amazing part is the video lessons are instructed by the author of those books. If you're trying to sell courses, subscription products or video series then the funnel of Mentor Box will be the best one to reverse hack.

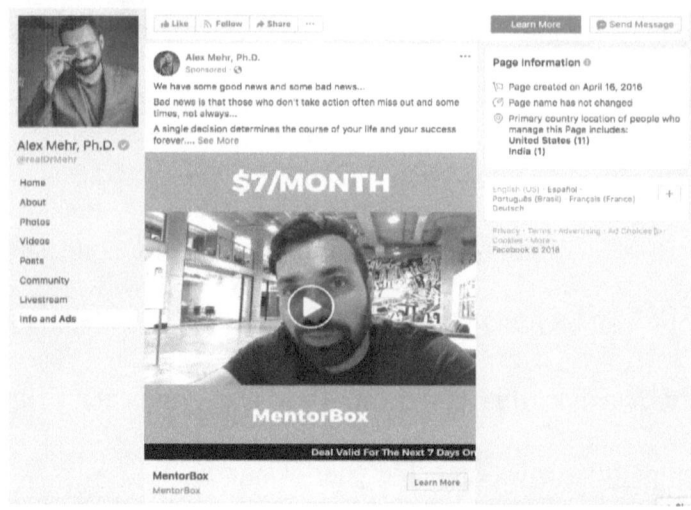

Analyze their headlines, videos and Call to Action (CTS) of their landing page.

Offers are crucial in every marketing funnels once you analyze your competitors landing page, look deeper into what they're trying to sell. Is it a physical product? Is it a subscription product or service? Is it an expensive or cheap product? What pricing strategy are they using?

In the case of Mentor Box first they tell their website visitors to take a Free 3 day trial of their platform and after three days they will charge $7 per month.

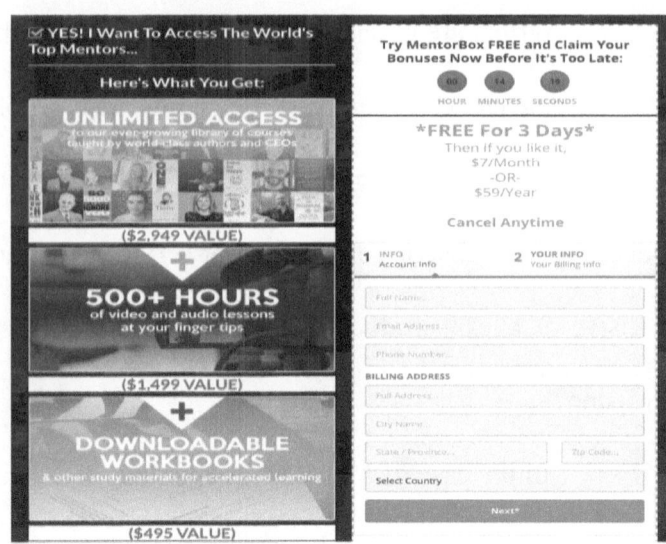

Don't forget to analyze their subtitles because they show you the different ways you can sell your products or services to your dream clients.

Backend funnel hacking is the most important and difficult part of the funnel hacking process. The backend of the sales funnel is where the higher revenue is generated these are the highest offers that your competitors provide for their clients.

When it comes to Mentor Box if you enroll

in their $7 per month subscription, they will show you an offer to join the Entrepreneurs academy.

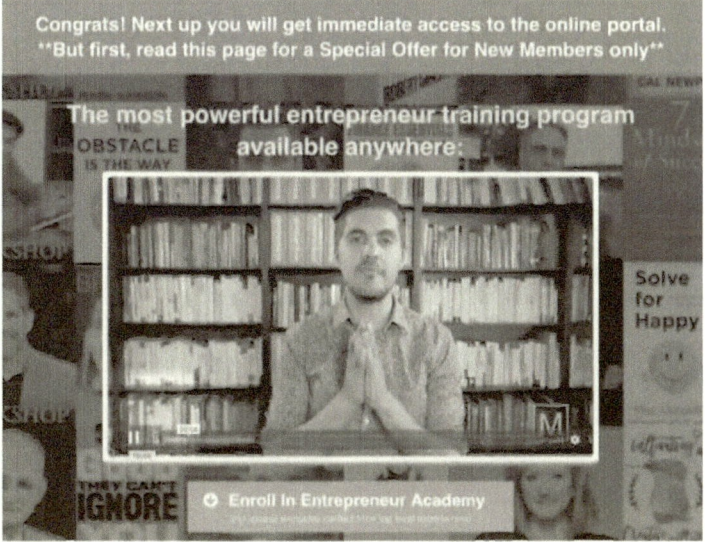

If you decline the offer and scroll down to the bottom of the page and click the 'no thank you' button, then you can see another offer to join a $99 product.

Imagine If You Learned Advanced Business Lessons From The Best Business Minds In The World

For a limited time we can offer a grant of $500 to help new members take advantage of this opportunity.

REGULAR PRICE: $1,000
Previous Offer: $199
Grant Credit: $100

Final Amount Due: $99

○ YES! I Claim My Grant And Want To Enroll
$99 with 30-day money-back guarantee

If you decline that offer, then you will be taken with another offer to purchase a monthly subscription for physical box membership.

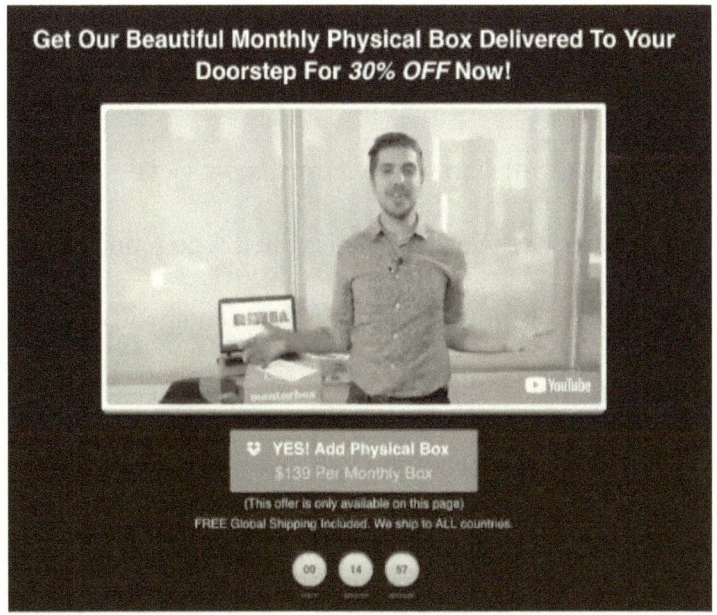

And this goes on….

In the funnel of Mentor Box, there are two main purchase flows one is set for clients who buy each upset and one for people who decline to buy. Analyzing the entire process of a funnel will help you to understand your competitors' products or services which offers lifetime value.

Retargeting Ads

You might have noticed after visiting some website you will start to see their ads on social networks and in other news feeds. This is called retargeting ads. If you see these types of ads of your competitors, then make sure to note them.

Some websites retarget their clients after joining their mailing list and some other retrofit peoples who visit any pages of their website make sure you differentiate each of them when you note these ads.

Marketers commonly use these types of ads to haunt their visitors to complete the act in which they left off. It can be a checkout process, buying a product or services from a sales page, etc.

TIP: You can install Facebook pixel on your website and create a Dynamic marketing campaign to create retargeting ads. If you like to create a retargeting ad on Google then install Google Remarketing tag on your website and create a remarking campaign.

Email Sequences

Once you sign up on your competitors' website makes sure to note all emails which are hitting your inbox to keep you on the right track to buy more products and services from them. Smart businesses have a sequence of follow-up emails in every part of their funnel to guide their clients. You can use these emails to create your own email sequence for your business.

SECRET #13

Sales Funnel Examples

In this chapter, we will discuss some of the best examples of sales funnels and how you can use them in your business.

The Free Book + Shipping Funnel

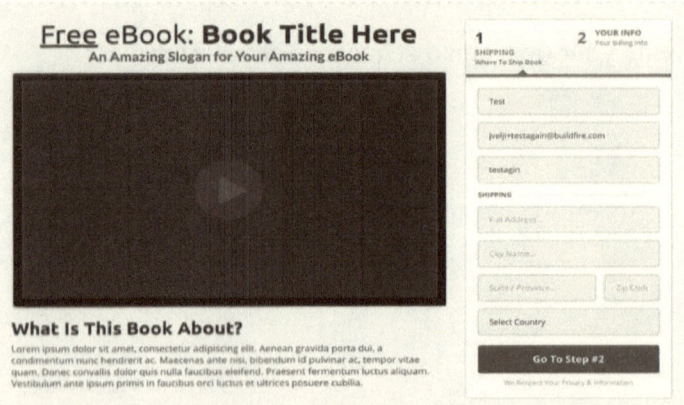

When you have a book published, even if it's not a bestseller, it still creates a certain amount of perceived authority. One of the best ways to sell your book and to collect email addresses to use the latter on your adventure is by creating free book funnels, it is one of the best sales funnels that have high conversion rates.

Selling your book on Amazon is good for sales, but there is high competition and you won't get the email of the peoples who buy your book. So the best alternative is offering your e-book or paperback for free while the clients pay for shipping. This method will help you to sell thousands of copies while covering all of your costs, including the amount you spend on advertisements. It will not generate much profit, but it definitely generates a good amount of leads and it will help you in your future adventures.

Fishbowl Funnel or Giveaway Funnel

One of the best ways to capture leads is by a giveaway funnel. You can use these leads to sell your products or services down the road. If you have a well-optimized giveaway funnel, then you will end up creating a massive amount of leads. One of the problems which come with giveaway leads is, people always like free stuff so you might get a lot of wrong audiences along with the right ones. One of the best ways to avoid this is by offering a price that is only needed by your target audience.

Simple Coach, consultant & Agency client generating funnel

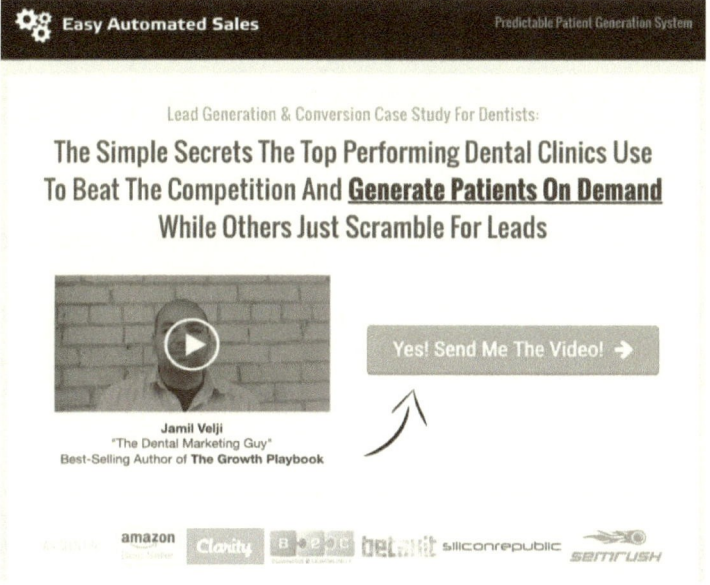

These sales funnels will be the best choice for peoples who are in consulting, coaching or agency business. This funnel will help you to take your leads to a quick sales call.

There are 4 steps in this funnel:

Valuable offer: In this step you will offer something valuable to your dream clients In the above case we're targeting dentists, to solve one of their main problems "Generating new clients" The above offer provides free video lessons about how to get more patients.

Deliver: Step two of their funnel is to deliver the offer which you offered your dream clients the above case I offered a video lesson that acts as a video sales letter. Once they get the video I will point them towards the next step.

Application: This is the application that your dream clients should fill up so that we will get a good idea about what they really want so that our time will not be wasted over a phone call. Once they fill up the pieces of information, they can book a call directly to you or wait for someone to contact them from your organization.

Call to book: Once your clients had filled up the application they can book or schedule a phone call in their preferred time on your calendar.

SECRET #14

The Purple Cow

After reading the title of this chapter you might be wondering what a purple cow is? In short, a purple cow is something that is worth talking about, something that's remarkable. I know most of the marketers out there are still struggling with the term purple cow. The concept of a purple cow was introduced by one of the top marketers in the world **Seth Godin** he had described it very well in his bestselling book **Purple Cow: Transform your business by being remarkable**. The book was published in 2002.

We're living in an era of noise where people have a lot of choices and less time. If you know the social media numbers, then you might know the organic reach of Facebook is shrinking to 1%, when people log in to Facebook there are more than 2500 ads competing to appear in your news feed and the click-through rate of the ads is decreased to 5%, These numbers show that it's extremely hard to stand out from the competition if you're not remarkable. In the era of a lot of choices and less time the reaction of normal peoples will be ignoring pieces of stuff, that's what's going to happen if your business is not remarkable.

The Purple Cow

Imagine you're driving to a new place and you pass a field of cows. For most persons, it's not a big thing because seeing a cow in a field is common, so we will ignore it and move forward, but imagine you're driving and you see a purple cow in s field what will you do? You will notice it since it captures your interest and most often you will stop your vehicle and take pictures with it and share the picture in social networks and your friends will like, comment and share your post since none of them ever seen a purple cow in their lifetime.

The average businesses are like black and brown cows that we don't notice since it's common. Being perfect is not remarkable.

Remember this Truth:

The opposite of remarkable is very good - Seth Godin

The ordinary cows can do something once in a while to grab your attention, but the attention which a purple make is a whole different story. The purple cow business is the businesses that are creative, more innovative and do things differently. The Purple cow business is remarkable and peoples often feel the need to inform their friends about it these types of businesses are easy to market and it provides word of mouth marketing which is insane and more powerful than other marketing strategies. The businesses which follow the purple cow strategy go viral in no time.

If you're from a marketing field you might know the 4 P's of marketing, if you don't know those are: Price, Product, Promotion, and Place. But Seth Godin had introduced to a new P in marketing and that's the Purple Cow and it stands for being remarkable.

DARE TO BE DIFFERENT

To be a Purple cow create remarkable products and services which the right persons seek, create a business that speaks out itself and which provides value for the right people they follow. Most people think to be the best or perfect is good, but in the real world no one cares about them so be different don't be too good or perfect instead of that try to be a purple cow to stand out of the competition. One of the best ways to be the leader in your market is being remarkable.

All customers are different, so differentiate your customers into two and find the customers that are most profitable for your business these customers will be 10 to 15% of your total customers. Find those customers delight them, encourage them, or surprise them, make them happy, that's how sneakers are born as Godin likes to call them.

In today's digital world, everything changes in minutes technology are evolving every day, Seth Godin encourages you to put a purple cow into everything you build to make it remarkable.

Bottom of the line my advice is to **BE first. Be Bold, Be**

Different.

CONCLUSION

Phew!

Right now, you may be feeling excited and proud of yourself since you had just completed a full course on marketing your business online. Right now, you know the strategies and tools to market your products and services online now you have to put your business in front of your right audience so that every traffic you get will be converted to sales.

This book is a marketing playbook. Don't just read it once and keep it on your shelf, carry it with you on your organization and refer it whenever you need it. I would suggest you take some time to implement the strategies which you learned from this book. I had given this book for reading too many peoples before it went public and many of them wanted me to look into their business personally to find and solve the problems which they're facing on their adventure. Once this book is valuable to billions. I know I can't help everyone. So I had created a special platform for the readers of this book called kiranrkg.com where you can contact me personally and I and my team will contact you back to solve the marketing problems you're facing.

With a lot of happiness. I'm finishing this book, thank you for reading and I wish you all success.

Kiran R.K.G